Here's One I Made Earlier

BBC

Foreword by
Valerie Singleton

Kyle Books

Here's One I Made Earlier

Contents

Craft

Cookery

Foreword by Valerie Singleton 6

Toys & Games

Christmas

Foreword
by Valerie Singleton
Blue Peter presenter 1962-1972

My years on *Blue Peter* were very special and great fun. Every day was so different. One moment I would be taking a baby lion for a walk... next flying a plane, then powerboat racing on the River Thames... going on Royal Safari with the Princess Royal... and who will ever forget Lulu the baby elephant. I certainly won't! And there will always be an important place in my heart for *Blue Peter's* unexpected and inspiring makes and bakes.

Who would have thought you could create a cat bed from a washing up bowl, design a doll's house from an old shoe box or make a flower pot from a margarine tub – all on live television! *Blue Peter's* ability to transform ordinary household items and old packaging into fun toys, gifts and games has captured viewers' imaginations for 60 years.

Christopher Trace and I made the very first *Blue Peter* Advent Crown in 1965. Made from just four wire coat hangers and some tinsel, who'd have guessed it would become the cult classic that it is today!

I hope you enjoy looking back at some of these activities as much as I have. Of course, no *Blue Peter* 'make' is complete without some sticky back plastic and saying together –'**Here's one I made earlier**'. Enjoy!

Valerie Singleton

CHRISTMAS GLITTER

JUNK JEWELLERY

MARBLE CASTLE

MARGARET PARNELL
Queen of Makes

The makes on *Blue Peter* were (and still are) a very important part of the programme. Most of the 'makes' were devised by Margaret Parnell. Her connection with *Blue Peter* began in 1963 when she wrote to the presenter Valerie Singleton with an idea for dolls' hats made of crepe paper. To her surprise, this idea was immediately taken up, then followed by 700 further 'makes', all created in the shed at the bottom of Margaret's garden.

Her most famous 'make', apart from Tracy Island was, of course, the advent crown made out of wire coat hangers which still features as part of our Christmas celebrations. When Margaret retired her creative crown was passed onto Gillian Shearing, who had been working in the Correspondence Unit replying to the thousands of letters into the programme. Today, with the benefit of the digital age, the *Blue Peter* team spot interesting trends that can be turned into makes, still using items around the home (with some imagination) to save our viewers that all important pocket money.
Ewan Vinnicombe, Editor Blue Peter

Margaret says: '*I'm so pleased to see my creations take on a new life in this book. I had such fun and each make brings back so many memories for me. At one time my personal favourite was the toy theatre but Tracy Island, which was, of course, the most famous and talked about, is now my favourite. In fact, just last week, I made a new one to fill in a few spare hours.*'

Here's One I Made Earlier

Craft

An unusual pencil case

It's easy to turn an old plastic bottle into a smart pencil case. All you need is an empty bottle, some enamel paint, a strip of cardboard, a small cork and some glue. Any bottle tall enough to take pencils is suitable. The first thing to do is to paint it white. The paint will go on better if you scratch off some of the printing with steel wool or sandpaper first.

Making the lid

When the paint is dry,

1. Cut all round about $\frac{1}{2}$ inch from the top of the main part of the bottle.
2. Cut a strip of cardboard $\frac{3}{4}$ inch deep, and long enough to fit round the lid.
3. Join ends together to form a circle, using glue or sticky paper.
4. Slip it on to lid. If it fits well, glue it firmly on. Fill in the hole in the lid with a small cork.
5. Paint the lid red, leaving the rim white.

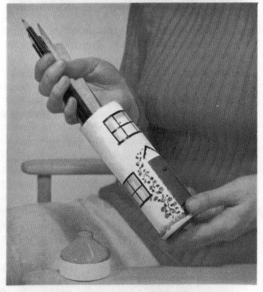

When you've decorated the outside of the bottle, the case is ready to be filled. You'll be surprised how much it will hold.

more things to make from plastic bottles

Here are some more things you can make out of plastic bottles. You can cover them with sticky backed plastic instead of painting them, and use cut-out pictures for decorations.

The spill box is the simplest of them all. Just cut off the top of your plastic bottle. For mine I used dark emulsion paint so that the cut-outs would show up more clearly.

I expect you remember when we made the money-box pig. His feet are corks cut and sandpapered to the right size and shape. His nose is made by filling the top of the bottle with plastic filler or plasticine, and his tail is a twisted piece of pipe cleaner. Before you paint him, cut a slit in his back for your money, and when the paint is dry, put on his eyes and ears. They're made out of felt and stuck on.

The cotton-wool holder makes a very useful present. I covered the bottle with sticky backed plastic, and the decoration at the top is a rosette of ribbon held together and secured to the lid with a paper fastener.

Another idea is to trim the bottle with lace. I took the flower cut-out from an old birthday card. You could use these bottles for bath salts, too.

FOOTBALL FAN

Are you a football fan too? With a home-made rattle like mine you can give your team some deafening applause every time they score. Make it from cheap off-cuts from a wood shop, and paint it in your team colours for a really professional finish.

1 To make the rattle you will need :
A piece of broom handle, 9″ long × 1″
4 blocks of wood, 2″ square × 1″ thick
2 pieces of wood, 9″ × 2″ × ½″
2 pieces of plywood, 9″ × ¾″ × ⅛″

2 With a drill the same diameter as the broom handle, make a hole through the centre of two of the square blocks of wood.

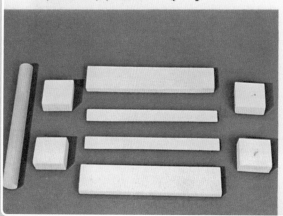

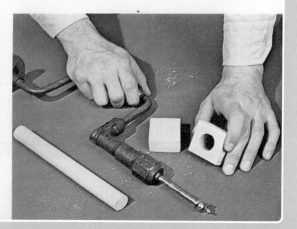

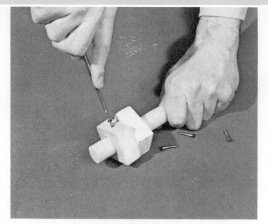

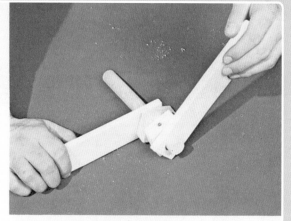

3 Push the squares over the broom handle so that the corner of one block is across the flat side of the other. If necessary glue and screw to the handle for a tight fit.

4 Drill a hole at one end of each of the two flat pieces of wood. They should spin freely when you fit them on the handle.

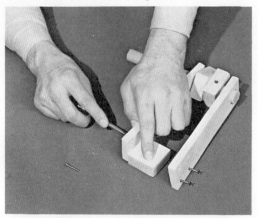

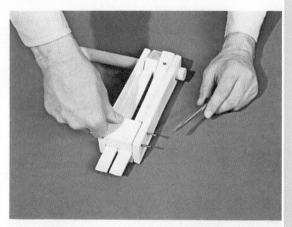

5 After testing for spin, fix them apart with one of the 2″ × 2″ × 1″ blocks of wood. Make sure you screw the block flush to the edges of the top and bottom pieces of wood.

6 Lay the two strips of plywood on the block and sandwich them in place with the second block. Test for maximum rattle.

7 Screw right through the top block into the second block to keep the plywood firmly in place. Trim off the ends of the plywood.

8 Paint the rattle in your team's colours. Mine's blue and white because I'm a Spurs supporter.

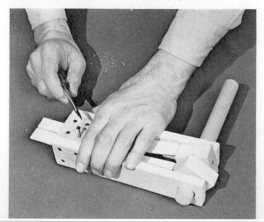

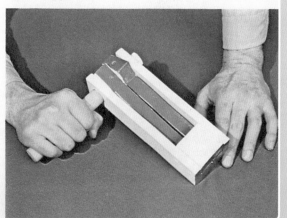

FLOWER TUBS

Growing bulbs is easy, and planted in home-made pots they make very special presents. Why not find some old plastic containers and make tubs like mine?

1 Margarine, honey, or peanut butter tubs are just right for little flowers like crocuses or a single hyacinth. I've decorated one by covering it completely with sticky-backed plastic.

The other I've left plain, but I've cut some flowers from a scrap of sticky-backed plastic and used them for a decoration.

When you've decorated the flower tubs, they make good holders for small pot plants, plastic flowers, or best of all, real bulbs that you can plant yourself.

2 Cut the top off a plastic squash bottle and you'll find the bottom part makes a good flower pot. One idea for decoration is to paint it with gloss or emulsion paint. When the paint is dry, decorate your flower pot with pictures cut from old birthday or Christmas cards.

Another idea is to cover the outside completely by glueing on split peas. A coat of clear varnish makes them shine and helps to keep them firmly on the flower tub.

3 This tub is the bottom of a half-gallon plastic can—the kind the washing-up liquid comes in. I've decorated it with string. Start by putting glue round the top of the can and winding the string gently round it. Add more glue and more string bit by bit until the can is completely covered. I've finished mine off by glueing a plait of string right round the top.

HOW TO PLANT BULBS

1 Start by putting some little stones, or pieces of broken flower pot, on the bottom of the tub. This will act as drainage.

2 Damp some special bulb fibre and fill the tub nearly to the top.

3 Press each bulb firmly down on the fibre and then cover them with more fibre, but leave the tip showing.

When you've finished planting, put the bulb tub in a dark, airy place—like the cupboard under the stairs. Don't use the airing cupboard. Bulbs grow best somewhere not too warm. Check every now and then that the fibre is still dampish, but don't water too much or the bulb will rot. Bulbs take about six to ten weeks to come through. When you see that the shoots are well through, bring them out into the light. In only a day or two the shoots will turn green and very soon after that you should have a handsome plant.

Bedtime for Jason

Jason likes luxury, and we make sure he gets it. Every night we put him to bed in a washing-up bowl. But it's no ordinary bowl. We've converted it into a super luxury softly padded bed. Here's how to make one just like it.

First of all, stand the washing-up bowl on a piece of foam plastic and draw all round it. Cut out the shape and you will find it fits into the bottom of the bowl. Then, lay an oblong of material inside the bowl and let the edges overlap enough to allow for a hem all round. There will be too much material at the corners, so cut away the extra pieces. Next, make a hem big enough to take a length of elastic, then lay the material down wrong side up and pin the foam plastic shape right in the centre. Sew it firmly into place and then run the length of elastic through the hem on the material and tie the ends in a knot. Now you will have a padded washable cotton cover that you can slip over the washing-up bowl to convert it into a pet's super bed. The elastic will hold it firmly in place under the rim.

Cats like Jason will love their new bed, and so will kittens, puppies, or even small dogs.

MAKE A DOOR STOP

Have you ever wanted to keep a door open? Most doorstops are expensive, but mine's an old brick in disguise, and it'll keep the heaviest door ajar.

1 All you need, besides your brick, is foam plastic, covering material, glue, and a needle and cotton—and if you've any spare wool, you can decorate the top with a woolly ball kitten.

2 Lay the brick on the foam plastic and draw guide lines. Cut out what you need and stick on to the brick. You can see how I've cut the foam to the exact shape of the brick.

3 The top of your brick will probably have a dip in it—you can feel this through the foam. Lay the brick flat in the middle of the material, dip uppermost.

4 Fold the material neatly round the brick, tucking in all the corners, and sew into place. The seam will not show as it will be the base of the doorstop. You can use the doorstop plain, or add a decoration like the woolly kitten.

5 The kitten is made from five different-sized woolly balls. You can use two or three colours so that it looks like a tabby or a tortoiseshell, or a single colour like this to match your material. Put the woolly balls together in this order. The tail is plaited strands of wool.

6 Fluff the woolly balls and the tail with a wire brush so that they look like fur. Sew them together with matching wool and add felt eyes and ears. The whiskers are strands of wool and the nose a triangle of felt. A ribbon bow and a bell give an attractive finishing touch.

Do you remember the day Lesley had toothache and had to stay in bed? I took over making these necklaces and bracelets, and although they look better on Lesley than they did on me, I really enjoyed making them. For one thing, they're dead easy, and for another, they needn't cost anything because you don't have to buy expensive materials. That's why I've called the necklaces and the bracelets that go with them "Junk" jewellery.

Decide how long you want your necklace to be. The "beads" are made from squares of silver kitchen foil (old foil will do if you clean it) and you'll need about 60 squares (7 cm each) for a necklace approximately 30 cm long. It's a good idea to use your first square as a pattern for all the others, but if you want smaller or larger beads, you can vary the size of your squares of foil. To make a bead, crumple a square and roll it round and round between the palms of your hands. You can flatten any sharp pieces or bumps with your fingernails. The idea is to make each ball as round and firm as possible.

Cut a length of thread about half as long again as you want your necklace to be—the extra is to allow for tying the knots. Use a needle with a large enough eye to fit fairly thick, strong thread through, and one with a fairly blunt end. Push it firmly through each bead. Thread enough beads until you've got the length you want your necklace to be—remember you've allowed extra thread at the end!

You can either leave your necklace silver or colour it by using paint. Painting's a bit messy, so make sure you put some paper on the table, and have a rag soaked in turpentine to wipe your hands on. If you remember to thread the beads loosely, you'll find you can get your paint brush in between the beads.

When you leave the beads to dry, hang them up so they don't stick to anything! You can paint the beads different colours to match your dresses. You can thread alternate large and small beads, or paint the beads with alternating colours. Small white beads next to large red ones look quite effective.

You can make matching bracelets in the same way, but thread them on thin elastic so they slip easily on to your wrist.

Lesley was delighted with her new jewellery— it even made her forget her toothache! And this junk jewellery would be ideal for the summer— it's so light it weighs almost nothing in a suitcase and you could even wear it when you went swimming and it wouldn't spoil.

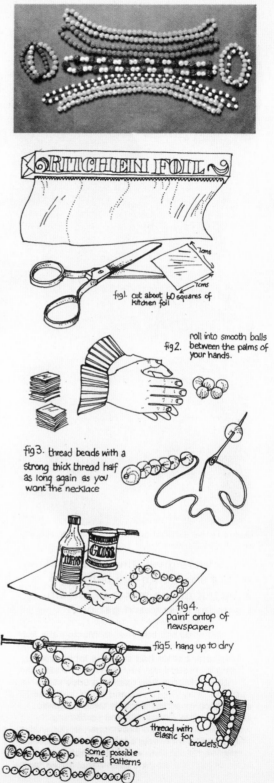

fig 1. cut about 60 squares of kitchen foil

fig 2. roll into smooth balls between the palms of your hands.

fig 3. thread beads with a strong thick thread half as long again as you want the necklace

fig 4. paint ontop of newspaper

fig 5. hang up to dry

thread with elastic for bracelets

some possible bead patterns

POSTCARD TABLE MATS

Here's an idea for a quick and easy present – and a cheap one, too. These mats would brighten up any tea table, and you can use them for cups and saucers as well as glasses.

Materials :
Picture postcards or pictures from magazines.
Cardboard – e.g. soap packet card.
Glue.
Top of a jar (pattern).
Sticky-backed transparent plastic or clear varnish.
Sticky-backed velour or felt scraps.
Box to put mats in.
Sticky-backed plastic with a pattern to cover the box.

Method :
1 Find a round lid to use as a pattern. You can choose whatever shape you prefer. Square or oblong mats are just as interesting, provided you can find something to make the pattern with.
2 Select the pictures you wish to make the mats with. You can use picture postcards, pictures from magazines, seed catalogues, or birthday cards.
3 Place the lid on the picture, selecting the piece you prefer.

4 Draw round the pattern. Cut out where drawn.
5 Using the same pattern, cut out two pieces of card which will form the reinforcement. (Choose a thin card as it is easier to cut and doesn't blunt the scissors).
6 Glue the three pieces together like a sandwich, making sure that any writing on the card faces inwards.
7 Using the pattern once again, cut out a piece of transparent sticky-backed plastic, and a piece of sticky-backed velour. The transparent plastic will make it easier to wipe marks off the mat.

8 Fix these to the card sandwich which you have already made.

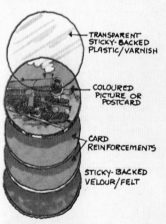

TRANSPARENT STICKY-BACKED PLASTIC/VARNISH

COLOURED PICTURE OR POSTCARD

CARD REINFORCEMENTS

STICKY-BACKED VELOUR/FELT

9 If you can't get hold of sticky-backed plastic or velour, the mats are just as effective finished off with varnish on the top and add patches of felt underneath.
10 For a final touch you could select a box to cover with sticky-backed plastic, or paint in a bright colour. Then put the mats inside. Remember it's easier to choose the box first and then make the mats.
11 If you have a spare picture, the box will look really nice if you stick a matching picture of your set of mats on the front, e.g. flowers, animals or places.

You've run out of pocket money and can't afford to buy presents? Fear not—these Handy Holders are the answer! Nine small wooden clothes pegs will transform one old yogurt pot into a present to be proud of. Here's the secret:

HANDY HOLDERS

Small Holder

1 Wash an empty yogurt pot and paint inside *and* out with enamel paint.
2 Take the springs from nine wooden clothes pegs by twisting the two wooden parts in opposite directions.
3 Glue the half clothes pegs to the pot; keeping the smooth tapering ends of each peg at the bottom and spacing the pegs a little apart at the top. After glueing about four or five pegs, leave them to dry, then continue until the whole pot is covered. When all the pegs are glued on, gently sandpaper them smooth and paint with clear varnish.
4 To make a top, use a lid from a cream cheese container, paint it with the enamel paint and cover the centre part with sticky-backed plastic.

Tray Holder

Cut off the bottom part of a soap-powder packet and cover with pegs glued close together—leaving no spaces.

Tall Holder

1 Cut off the bottom of a washing-up liquid container and paint inside and out.
2 Glue a circle of pegs around the bottom of the container with the *flat smooth end* of the peg at the *top*.
3 Glue a second circle of pegs around the top of the pot, with the flat smooth ends of the pegs *downwards*, overlapping the top of the first circle and allowing the top of the pegs to stand above the top of the container.

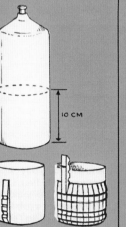

10 CM

Tin Holder with Lid

(Useful for biscuits)
1 Paint the outside of a dried milk tin and glue a circle of pegs around the *top* of the tin.
2 Overlap with a bottom circle of pegs below the bottom of the tin.
3 Cover the middle of the tin's lid with sticky-backed plastic. Make a hole in the middle of the lid and fix a saucepan lid handle. Paint handle with enamel paint.

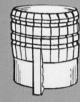

Take Hart if you want to draw our Blue Peter Ship!

Tony Hart designed the ship back in 1963. Since then it's appeared on well over a million badges! Here's Tony's ingenious method of drawing our symbol.

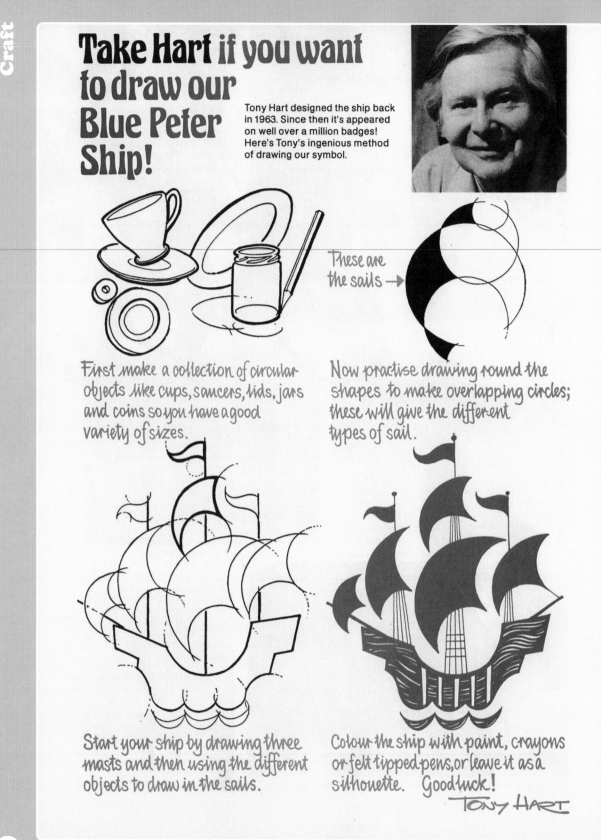

These are the sails →

First make a collection of circular objects like cups, saucers, lids, jars and coins so you have a good variety of sizes.

Now practise drawing round the shapes to make overlapping circles; these will give the different types of sail.

Start your ship by drawing three masts and then using the different objects to draw in the sails.

Colour the ship with paint, crayons or felt tipped pens, or leave it as a silhouette. Good luck!

TONY HART

'Ear 'Ear

A cheap and cheerful way to cheat the wintery weather!

1 Wind chunky wool over a piece of thick card – don't overlap the strands.

5cms

← 12cms →

✂ Cut through the strands down one side of the card.

2 Measure a strand of wool 60cm long and knot one end.

3 Take a length of the wool cut from the card and fold it in half so that it forms a loop. (If you're using thin wool use more than one strand at a time).
Slip the loop under the long piece of wool and bring the ends over it and down through the loop.

Pull the ends tightly and push the strand down the length of wool to the knotted end.

4 Continue to tie on strands of wool, bunching them tightly together, for just over half the length of wool.

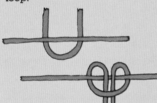

Tie a knot in the long length of wool to hold the strands secure, and cut off the spare wool.

5 Using matching thread, sew the length of knotted strands into a flat, round shape. Starting at one end of the knotted strand, turn it into a tiny circle, securing the shape with fairly large stitches.

Continue spiralling the knotted edge round, and stitching it in position, until the whole length is sewn into a round shape. Keep all the wool strands facing away from the stitching. Firmly oversew the stitches at the end of the spiral.

6 Make a second ear-muff in the same way and trim with scissors. Tug the muffs slightly at the ends to give them an oval shape. You can use a teazle or suede brush to fluff up the wool.

7 Cut twelve strands of wool long enough to reach across the top of your head to the middle of your ears. Tie together at one end and plait loosely in three groups of four strands.

Tie another piece of wool at the end to stop the plait unwinding.

8 Pin the ends of the plait to the inside of each ear-muff, checking they fit across your head and over your ears properly, then oversew the plait firmly in position.
To hold your ear-muffs in place, thread some thin elastic through the bottom edge, and adjust the length so that the muffs fit close to your ears. Tie the ends of the elastic firmly.

P.S. To keep both ears warm, you only need 40g of wool.

DRESSING

2 As you work on the wig you'll find the string fluffs out even more, giving a hairy look. Any ends that don't fluff out can be opened up with your fingers. The wig can be left its natural blonde colour or dyed. Use a cold-water dye according to the instructions on the tin – half a tin should be enough.

10 cm

DYE

String wigs

1 For a punk look, cut off 10 cm lengths of sisal string, separate the strands and tie on the string just like the wool. Because the ends fray, it's easier to fold the strand and push the folded part through the mesh. Open it out before tying in place.

P.S. You can make dolls' wigs using the same method. The wig will fit your doll better if you thread thin elastic round the lower edge, tying the ends to fit the head. Pull the wool strands down to cover any elastic that shows.

CHIN FACES

DRESSING UP

THE three faces at the bottom of the previous page, take the prize for our spookiest experience of the year! Rebecca Patterson and her cousins, Joanna and Harriet Amos, had the idea during the holidays. Harriet was chatting to the others lying on the bed with her head hanging down. "We thought her chin would look just like a nose if we painted two eyes above it," explained Rebecca. So they experimented and came up with Chin Faces!

It couldn't be simpler to turn a friend into a Chin Face. Here's how Rebecca, Joanna and Harriet transformed Peter:

1 Lie back on a bed or sofa and hang your head over the edge.

2 Hold a piece of material over your face, covering it from your nose to the top of your head.

3 Using face paints, get a friend to draw eyes and two nostrils on your upside-down chin.

4 Bits of wool make effective "hair." When you start to move your chin and talk, the effect is hilarious!

WOBBLEY

Here's an unusual way of supporting your team without spending a fortune! Our Wobbley Bobblies can be made in any colour combination and you can either pin them on your coat or make a whole family and decorate your room with them.

The secret ingredient is a simple woolly ball – and if you've never made one, here's a quick reminder.

Caterpillar Wobbley Bobbley

Make one ball for the head and six slightly smaller ones for the body – three in the same colour as the head and three more in your second colour.

To join the balls together, start with the tail end and thread a large needle and wool through the centre of each ball up to the head. Go back through the head and the other balls to the tail. Tie the two ends of wool together and cut off the spare wool.

Quick woolly ball

4 strands of wool to completely cover card 4 times

Cut wool from card around edge

Tie knot

Tie knot

The face: The eyes are two or three circles of felt or coloured paper, stuck to the head. You can use 2p, 1p and ½p pieces as patterns. Glue the smaller circles on to the larger and stick them into position on the head.

BOBBLIES!

The Hat: The hat is a piece of plain knitting. Cast on about 36 stitches on size 4 mm (No.8) needles. Knit two rows in one colour, then two rows in the second colour until you have five stripes. Don't cast off but thread the wool through the stitches on the needle. Pull up the wool to gather the stitches, then sew the hat together down the sides. OR you could use the top of an old sock!

Pull threaded wool and tie into knot

Cut top off sock

Sew end

Pull threaded wool and tie into knot

The small bobble on the hat is made by winding the wool around two fingers about thirty times. Tie in the centre, cut through loops and fluff out into a ball. Then glue to the top of the hat and glue the hat to the head.

Wind wool

Tie centre

Cut edges

Wobbley Bobbley

If you're short of wool, or you don't want to make so many woolly balls, you'll only need one ball for the Wobbley Bobbley.

Pipe-cleaner arms – wind wool round them to match colour of body and glue firmly into position.

Thin cardboard feet covered with felt matching the body.

CRAZY CRESS HEADS

Grow a Crazy Cress Head and you'll never be short of a sandwich filling! Every haircut gives you a snack – delicious with a hard-boiled egg or peanut butter.

HEAD

1 Loose woven cloth to allow the cress to grow through (if you use the knitted sort of dishcloth with two layers, trim off the edge all the way round and just use one layer).

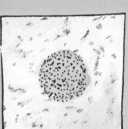

Lay the cloth flat. Sprinkle half a teaspoon of cress seed in the middle, in a circle.

2 Roll up four sheets of kitchen roll paper into a loose ball. Place it on the seeds very carefully without disturbing them.

3 Bring the corners up over the paper ball, bunching them together. Secure the bunch close to the paper ball with an elastic band (it doesn't matter if a few seeds drop through).

4 Fill a medium sized jar with water – a jam or pickle jar is ideal. Rest the head on the rim of the jar with the bunched material in the water.

5 Put the jar in a dark cupboard and leave it there until the seeds have begun to sprout (this will take 3 or 4 days). Take the jar out of the cupboard and stand it on a window sill. The leaves will be yellow at first, but after a couple of days they will turn green.

BODY

It can be tricky dressing the jar with water in it, so either dress another jar, or transfer the head into another jar and tip the water out of the original jar to dress it.

1 Cut away the foot and heel of an old sock and use the top of the sock to cover the jar.

2 Bring the cut edge of the sock over the top of the jar and tuck in any spare material. Bring the fold just below the rim (if it comes higher it will get wet from the head and absorb the water).

3 Half fill the jar with water and put the head in place.

FACE

1 Find the smoothest part of the head for the features. If there are any roots or leaves growing in the wrong place, just pull them out.

2 Cut shapes from felt or paper for the eyes and mouth. Simply press them onto the head (the damp material should hold them in position).

Once your Cress head has grown its cress 'hair' long enough you can give it a good hair cut and enjoy a snack!

ACCESSORIES

Use your imagination to turn your Cress Head into a character by adding a few buttons, a ruff, or perhaps a ribbon to the dress.

If you like, use kitchen foil for a space age Cress Head. Or, you could make a cheery red scarf from a tied handkerchief.

Dangly ear-rings can be made from small cut-up sections of a plastic drinking straw threaded together on a length of sewing thread and draped over the head.

You can make a pair of glasses by cutting the shape from a yoghurt pot. Colour them with a felt-tip pen and tie a piece of thin elastic at each side.

ALL TIED UP!

Going to a party and dying to be different? Make one of these designer ties to match your outfit! They're cheap, colourful and cardboard so they're light to wear and they make great presents.

BOW TIES

1. All you need is some stiff cardboard and some trimmings. Begin by laying a ruler on a piece of card and draw down both sides (a).

Draw two more lines (b).

3. To make the bow shape, draw from the corner to the centre line. When you have marked all four, you will see the shape of your tie on the card. Cut it out, and it's ready to decorate.

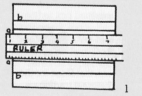

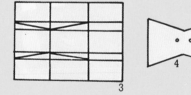

2. Decide how long you want your tie to be and draw a line across the card (a).

Measure the centre of your tie and draw another line across the card (b).

4. You can cover your tie with sticky-backed plastic, or use paints or felt tipped pens.

To fix the elastic, make two holes near the centre. Be careful doing this bit.

5. Use a length of elastic that's long enough to go round your neck comfortably plus a bit extra to tie a bow. Thread it through the holes and tie the bow, so that you can stretch the elastic enough to get it over your head.

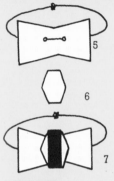

6. To hide the holes, cut out a cardboard "knot" shape and cover it with a piece of sticky-backed plastic.

7. To fix it, hold it in place on the tie and wrap a piece of sticky-backed plastic round to the back and press down firmly.
If you are painting your tie, glue the knot firmly in place and you'll get a very similar effect.

LONG TIES

1. Draw a tie shape on a piece of card, complete with knot. You can use the length of a ruler as a guide.
Start by drawing an oblong then mark the knot (a) and rule straight lines from the corners to the knot to make sure that the finished tie will look neat and symmetrical (b).

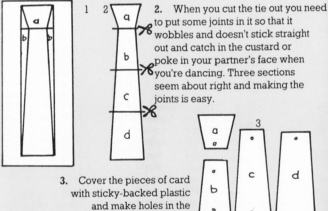

2. When you cut the tie out you need to put some joints in it so that it wobbles and doesn't stick straight out and catch in the custard or poke in your partner's face when you're dancing. Three sections seem about right and making the joints is easy.

3. Cover the pieces of card with sticky-backed plastic and make holes in the bottom of each piece.

4. The joints are ordinary paper clips — you can choose coloured ones to match the tie — and brass paper fasteners. Push the fasteners through the holes and through the clips and open them out. This not only makes a secure joint but a very good decoration too.

5. When you've fixed all the pieces, your tie will have an excellent wobble to it. And if you cover the backs of the paper fasteners with extra bits of sticky-backed plastic, the ends won't catch in your clothes.

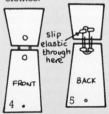

To fix a length of elastic to the tie you don't need to make any holes, just slip the elastic through the paper clip behind the knot.

You can make all kinds of ties in a whole variety of colours using this technique. Your own designer ties at a fraction of the cost in the shops!

BEASTIE BOXES

SICK of being ticked off because you're untidy? With a Beastie Box like these, you'll have a neat solution to a monster problem! Whether you feed them with model cars, puzzles, building bricks, or just use them as a waste paper basket, they'll lurk in the corner of your room waiting to be fed with all your odds and ends. Make them from rubbish and see how useful they'll be.

Cover a grocery box with sticky backed plastic on the *outside* — or paint it, if you prefer. Paint the *inside* a dark colour and make the front outside a dark colour, too.

Make the eyeballs from sticky paper circles. To make the eyes roll, lay one circle down — sticky side up — and lay a piece of cotton on it.

A THE EYE SOCKETS are sections cut from a toilet roll and painted black.

Sandwich the cotton right in the middle of the eye with another sticky white circle. Colour the centre red, with a felt tip pen or paint.

Leave the thread long, because it has to be threaded through the eye socket. Do this with a needle, just like sewing on a button, so that it hangs loose and wobbles in a revolting way. Stick the end down on the toilet roll with sticky tape. Fix the eyes on the box with sticky tape, too.

B THE MOUTH is made from half a plastic pot. Cut the pot in two. One half is just right to make the base for a mouthful of fangs.

C THE FANGS are cut from cardboard. Fix them in place in the mouth with sticky tape.

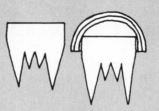

Fix the mouth and fangs on the box with sticky tape. You don't have to do this neatly, because it'll be covered with the Beastie's hair!

1 **THE HAIR FRINGES**
Wind the wool round a piece of cardboard. The size really doesn't matter, but make it wide enough so that the hair will hang down over the eyes and over the mouth. It doesn't matter if it is too long because you can trim it later. Wind the wool round the card loosely, so that you can slide it down, and make sure that the strands stay neatly side by side and don't overlap.

2 When you have a long enough piece, lay the card down and run a strip of double sided tape right along the length and press it down firmly.

3 Cut the wool off the card by snipping down the whole length on the *other* side of the card.

4 Now you have a fringe. If you cut down the length of the double-sided sticky tape, you'll have strips long enough for the moustache and the eyebrows.

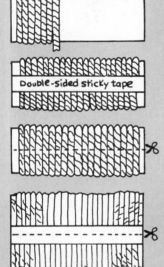

Double-sided sticky tape

5 Peel the backing off the sticky tape and stick the fringes in place. Trim the centre out of the eyebrows so you can see the Beastie glaring, and a bit off the moustache too, so that the fangs show through.

6 Cover the face in exactly the same way, by making more fringes. Use a different colour from the eyebrows and moustache. Start covering the face from the *bottom* and work upwards so that the fringes overlap each other.

7 **THE CLAWS**
For the final touch cut out some cardboard claws, and cover them with fringes in the same way. Stick the claws to the bottom of the box. You can give them shiny nails by covering the tips with shiny paper.

Finish your Beastie with a fringe stuck around the top edge of the box, for a really neat finish.

Each of the Beasties takes about half a ball of wool — the thickness and colour can be anything you like. No matter what you choose, they'll end up looking really horrible!

Cardigan Cushions

As any fan of 'Changing Rooms' will know, it's the accessories that make a room. And what about these funky cushions that could transform a boring bedroom into a cosy den? They cost a fortune to buy, but here's how to convert an old cardigan or jumper into a cushion that would turn Laurence Llewelyn-Bowen green with envy.

● **Lay an old cardigan out flat,** making sure the bottom edges are even. Do up the buttons. Use a ruler and a piece of chalk to draw a line from under one arm right across to the other. Carefully cut along this chalk line

● **You will be left with a kind of tube.** The cut edge will be the top of the cushion and that's why you have to make sure the bottom edges are absolutely even or your cushion will be wonky. If you can unravel part of the top half of the cardigan, you can use this wool for sewing.

● **Turn the tube shape inside out** so that the buttons are on the inside and pin together the edges you have just cut. Thread a bodkin or a big-eyed needle with some wool and sew these edges together to stop it unravelling. Small running stitches are best and two rows will make it really strong. Overstitch the bottom edge.

● **Undo one or two of the buttons** and turn the cushion right side out. You will already have the basic cushion shape and it's ready to be filled. You could use a stuffed pad from an old cushion or odds and ends, like the top half of your cardigan.

● **If you are using an old jumper the method is almost the same.** Simply cut off the top from underarm to underarm, turn inside out and sew the cut edges.

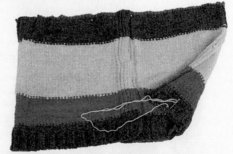

● **Turn it back to the right side out** but instead of sewing the bottom end of the jumper, cut or undo the stitching on both sides as far as the end of the ribbing. If necessary over-stitch these edges to prevent unravelling. On one side of your cushion shape, sew 5 or 6 buttons above the ribbing, spacing them equally. On the other bottom edge make some loops with matching or contrasting coloured wool. Space them to correspond with the buttons. Fill your cushion and tuck the button side under the pad and do up the buttons.

● **Tassels on the corners give the cushions a professional look** and they are easier than you'd think to make. All you need is a piece of cardboard and a long length of wool. The cardboard should be as wide as you want the tassel to be long. Simply wind the wool around the card roughly 15 times – the more wool, the thicker the tassel. Make a note of how many winds you do and wind the same amount for each tassel. Leave a long end before cutting the wool. Thread this end on to a needle and wrap it a couple of times around the wool in the middle of the card. Tie it firmly. Now slip the card out of the loop of wool. Hold the loop by the knot and cut through the end opposite the knot. To finish off the tassel, fold the two bunches of wool together and wind another piece of wool around it roughly 1 cm below the knot and fasten securely.

● Then put the threaded needle through the knot at the top and sew the tassel to the corner of the cushion.

SUPER FURRY ANIMAL COAT HANGERS

TO MAKE A FURRY COAT HANGER YOU WILL NEED:

- *a plastic coat hanger*
- *fun fur fabric (approx 33 x 60 cm for a dog, a little more for a long-eared rabbit and a little less for a chick)*
- *toy stuffing (kapok) or similar*
- *a button or felt for nose*
- *felt for tongue*
- *paper circles for eyes*
- *ribbon for bow*

1 To make a furry dog coat hanger, cover the main part of the plastic hanger with two strips of fur fabric. Each strip should be about 12 cm

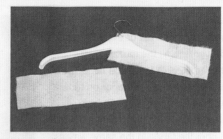

wide and long enough to reach from the hook to the end of the hanger plus a couple of extra centimetres to allow for the seams.

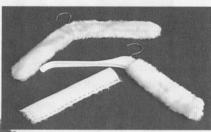

2 Fold the strips in half lengthways, wrong side out, then stitch the long sides of one piece together and one of the short ends. Don't worry if you aren't good at sewing as you don't have to do tiny neat stitches as they will sink into the fur and hardly show.

3 Stitch the second piece in the same way but before you stitch the short end, check that the pile on the fur runs downwards on both strips when seen from the front.

4 Turn the strips furry sides out and slip on to the hanger with the seams at the bottom. Fold in the raw edges a little way and stitch the two strips together.

5 The head is made from two circles of fur. Cut these out using a saucer and a medium sized plate for the patterns. The small circle will be the muzzle. Sew straight stitches around the edge then pull up the thread, leaving a hole in the middle. Over-sew to keep the gathers in place.

Pet Draught

Transform an old fleece jumper into a cosy cat or dog draught excluder. They'll look cute all year round even when there isn't an icy blast blowing under the door.

Blue Peter

You will need:

- an unwanted fleece jumper
- stuffing
- needle and thread
- coloured felt
- buttons
- a pipe cleaner
- a plastic milk bottle
- glue and wire bag ties

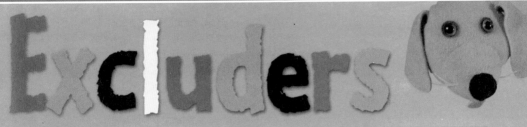

Excluders

1. Cut the sleeves off the fleece.

Turn one sleeve inside out and slide the other one inside so that the right sides of the fleece are facing each other.

2. To join the 2 sleeves sew around the cut edges using small running stitches. Oversew the last stitch and turn the sleeves to the right side. You will end up with a long tube shape.

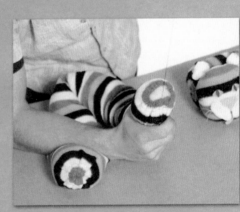

3. Close one end by stitching all the way around the edge and pull the thread so the material gathers up. Oversew.

4. Fill the tube shape with stuffing and close up this end as before.

Blue **Peter**

5. For the head, cut out a circle from leftover fleece. A 26cm plate makes a good template. Sew small stitches around the edge of the circle and pull the thread to gather up the fabric. Leave a small hole and push in stuffing to shape the head. Pull the thread tight and oversew.

6. To make a cat, cut a nose and tongue shape from pink felt. For the muzzle and cheeks, draw a large shape from white or light coloured felt. Eyes can also be cut from felt or you could use buttons.

Cut 2 ear shapes from the fleece and 2 more in light coloured felt. Glue a wire bag tie down the centre of each fleece ear and then stick the felt ear shapes on top.

Position all the facial features on the head and when you are happy glue them in place.

For whiskers, cut 3 very thin strips from a plastic milk bottle. Thread each whisker onto a large eyed needle and push through the muzzle from one side of the nose to the other.

7. Stitch the head onto the body. Use a black marker pen to draw a line from the bottom of the nose to the top of the tongue.

8. From the leftover fleece cut a piece 30 cm long by 8 cm wide which will become the tail. Lay stuffing on one half of the tail and put a pipe cleaner on top. Roll to form the tail shape and stitch or glue in place. Fold one end into a point and glue or stitch. Attach the other end of the tail to the body and you will end up with a finished cat draught excluder.

Blue Peter

9. If you want to make a dog – the muzzle is slightly different. Using a saucer as a pattern, cut out a circle from the fleece.

Cut the circle in half. You only need one half. Fold this in half, right sides facing, and sew the 2 straight edges together.

10. Turn the muzzle right sides out and fill the shape with a little stuffing. Sew or glue onto the head. Cut out a circle of black felt and cut a V shape from the edge to the centre. Pull the felt into a cone shape and carefully glue onto the end of the muzzle. The remaining features are the same as for the cat.

Blue **Peter**

Blooming Gorgeous!

Whatever you want to say – happy birthday, happy Easter or happy Mothers' Day – there's no better way than to say it with flowers! My idea for everlasting blooms in a pretty vase will save you pounds and is guaranteed to please.

All you need is:
- A small juice carton
- PVA Glue
- Paint
- Sawdust (available from pet shops)
- Thin wire
- Cereal packet
- Crepe paper
- Green card or paper
- Modelling clay
- Shredded tissue paper

Cut the top off an empty juice carton. Rinse and dry the carton and cut away 3.5 cm from the sides.

Cut thin card from a cereal packet to cover the outside of the carton.

Draw and cut away curved shapes on both the front and the back of the carton.

KONNIE HUQ
Blue Peter presenter 1997-2008

My favourite makes were always the ones involving action figures such as Sindy, Barbie or Action Man. I loved making the doll's dress shop for instance and would have fun naming the dolls and playing with them as I made stuff. I remember naming the shop assistant in the dress shop Chenise and the other doll was named Carmel after the studio floor manager that day! Making this type of thing was always fun as there were so many elements and little details and kids always love things in miniature. I can still remember making a fitted kitchen for my Sindy as a kid, complete with waste height units made from rectangular tissue boxes and a washing machine with a clear circular window which was the bottom of a Chambourcy chocolate mousse tub!

My ultimate favourite, of course, had to be Tracy Island, which I made when CBBC started running *Thunderbirds* again. I think I had remembered watching Anthea Turner make it first time round and was chuffed to be making something so iconic. I loved all the little details, such as the bendable pipe cleaner palm trees and that it was compatible with the shop bought *Thunderbirds* toys and, of course, a fraction of the price of buying the real thing!

My biggest disaster was when I was making an oven bake with two members of S Club 7 and didn't have an oven dish to put it in! On live telly you have to think on your feet with the crucial seconds ticking away as you near *Newsround* knowing you have to end the programme on time! I managed to get the crew to hunt one out and hand it into shot and speedily get to the 'Here's one I made earlier' version.

Children love making things and being creative and they love the clever ways in which the makes utilise everyday household objects and packaging and ingeniously transform into gifts and toys with a personal touch. What's not to love?!

Here's One
I Made Earlier

Cookery

Sweets for your Party

You can make these sweets in several different flavours and, with different decorations, they can look and taste exciting, and they don't need any cooking.

First of all, wash your hands and then collect all the things you need and put them on the kitchen table. You will want:

2 mixing bowls
a sieve
an egg-whisk
a pastry-board
a rolling-pin
a wooden spoon
a small wine-glass or an egg-cup or fancy cutters
grease-proof paper

and for the sweets:

1 lb. icing sugar
1 egg white·
1 teaspoon blackcurrant juice
glacé cherries for decoration

This is how you make the sweets:

1. Sieve nearly all the icing sugar into a bowl, keeping just a little in the packet for later use.
2. Whisk the egg white lightly in the other bowl until it is frothy, but not stiff, and then add the teaspoonful of blackcurrant juice.

Some of the other flavourings I used were coffee essence and peppermint oil. You can buy all kinds of different colourings at the grocer's and different flavourings too, so that you can have a whole rainbow of sweets at your next party. Do remember to wash your hands each time you change from one colour or flavour to another, so that you don't get the peppermint mixed with the coffee, or the pink with the blue.

3. Mix the sugar, the egg white and the black-currant juice together. This will be hard work. You can mix it with your fingers if you like till it is like modelling clay.

4. Sprinkle the pastry-board with the icing-sugar you have left in the packet. Then roll out your mixture on the board so that it is about half an inch thick.

5. Cut your sweets out, using the wine-glass or egg-cup, or fancy cutters if you have them. If the mixture sticks to the glass or cutter, rub a little icing sugar round the edge.

6. Put each sweet on to the greaseproof paper and decorate with a tiny piece of glacé cherry.

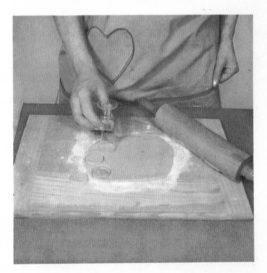

Now you must be patient and leave your sweets for twelve hours to dry. Put them in little paper cases so that they don't stick to each other and then arrange them in a chocolate box.

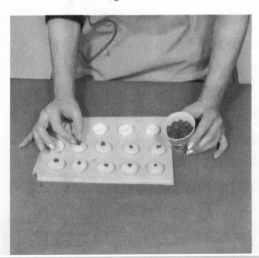

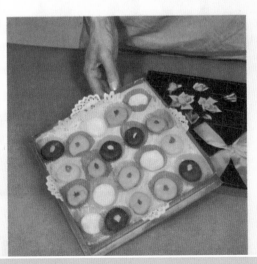

Fruit cream crunch

Even if you're no good at cooking, it's hard to go wrong with Fruit Cream Crunch. For one thing you don't have to use an oven, and although it looks so spectacular, it couldn't be more simple to make. And it's easy to vary the recipe to make it big or small according to how much fruit and cream you've got. For a six-inch plate size you will need: 3 oz. melted butter, 8 digestive biscuits, 2 tablespoons of sugar, 1 tin of your favourite fruit and some cream for decoration.

1
Crush the digestive biscuits into crumbs and put them into a bowl.

2
Add two level tablespoons of granulated sugar and stir.

3
Now melt 3 oz. of butter and add to the mixture.

4 Stir all the ingredients together until they are well mixed.

5 Grease your plate. You can use the greaseproof wrapper from the butter for this.

6 Spread the biscuit mixture evenly all over the plate about ½ in. thick. Leave somewhere cool for at least two hours.

7 While the mixture is left to harden, whip some cream or topping until it is stiff.

8 Put some fruit on to the biscuit mixture and cover with whipped cream or topping.

9 Decorate with the rest of the fruit. You could use raspberries, strawberries or blackberries.

10 Finish off the decoration with silver balls and chocolate flakes.

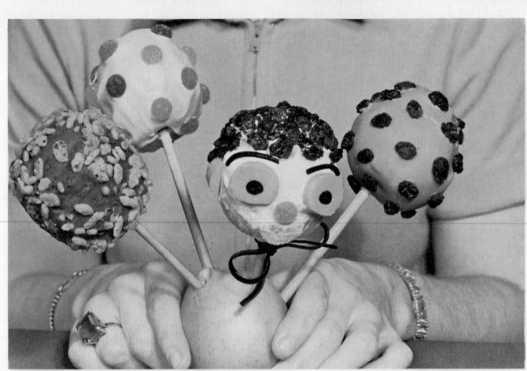

Chocolate apples

We didn't have these apples at the Hilton Hotel — but they're delicious to eat and extremely simple to make. As well as using different kinds of chocolate — plain, white or caramel — you can have different decorations, too. I've used rice krispies, jelly sweets, raisins and liquorice allsorts. This is how you make them:

1 After washing and drying your apple, push a clean wooden skewer through the centre. You can also use thin dowelling.

2 Break the chocolate into pieces in a bowl. You'll find that the plain chocolate is the easiest to melt.

3 Melt the chocolate by standing the basin in a saucepan or larger basin that has some warm water in it. Stir until smooth and runny.

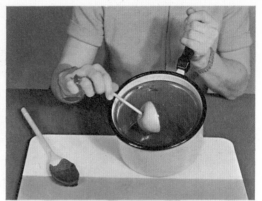

4 Dip the apple in the chocolate stirring it round to coat it well.

5 Next dip the apple in a bowl of rice krispies and put on greaseproof paper until the chocolate sets.

6 The creamy white type of chocolate looks good with small jelly sweets decorating it.

7 The caramel type of chocolate goes well with seedless raisins or you could use glacé cherries.

8 I made the clown's face from raisins and liquorice allsorts. You could also use chopped nuts, or desiccated coconut.

SWEET OR SAVOURY ?

When you invite your friends to tea, what sort of food do they prefer—the sweet things or the savouries? Here are some ideas that should please them all—stuffed dates, savoury eggs and tuna tomatoes. The radish roses and the sausage snacks will help to decorate the table.

Stuffed Dates

You will need: Dates and marzipan; green colouring, nuts; glace cherries and silver balls for decoration. You could also use chocolate chips, angelica or sugar strands. If you hate marzipan, substitute a mixture of equal quantities of butter and sugar creamed together.

Slit along one side of the dates (choosing the least squashy ones) and take out the stones. Divide the marzipan in half – leave half plain and colour the rest with a few drops of green essence or cochineal. Stuff the middles of the dates with marzipan. Decorate.

Savoury Eggs

You will need: Hard boiled eggs; margarine or butter; mayonnaise and seasoning. Parsley and paprika for decoration.

Cut the eggs in half. Mash the yolks with margarine, mayonnaise and seasoning. Fill the eggs with the mixture.

Radish Roses

You will need: A bunch of radishes and a bowl of cold water.
Wash the radishes and trim the stalks. Make 4 or 6 deep crisscross cuts in the top of each one – taking care not to cut right down to the bottom. Put them in a bowl of cold water – after a while they will open like flowers.

Sausage Snacks

You will need: Cold sausages, cheese, capers, cocktail sticks and a grapefruit.
Cut slices of cold sausage and cheese. Spear a slice of cheese, then one of sausage and another piece of cheese onto a cocktail stick. Finish off with a caper. Push the sticks into a grapefruit.

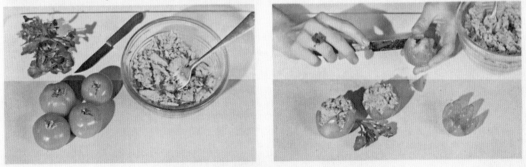

Tuna Tomatoes

You will need: Firm tomatoes (squashy ones are no good); tinned tuna fish (or you can use sardines or pilchards) and seasoning. Watercress for decoration. A sharp pointed knife.

Mash the tuna with the seasoning. Slice the tops off the tomatoes. Cut a dragon's tooth shape round the edge of each tomato. Scoop out the seeds and fill with tuna.

Celebration Cakes

Have you ever wanted a cake to celebrate a special occasion? Or for a particularly important tea party? This rose-decorated straw hat could be the answer! It's covered in a thick layer of creamy butter icing – I've flavoured mine with chocolate – but you can make yours any colour or flavour you like. Your friends will never guess that the "hat" started off as an ordinary 2/6d. sponge (or you could even bake the sponge base yourself if you had plenty of time) and the coloured roses give the cake a really professional look, like something produced at that smart hotel where John once learned how to be a waiter. But they're so simple that anyone could make them – even someone who's usually not at all good at cooking.

And if you don't want to make the straw hat, you can transform small cup cakes by decorating them with single roses – just like the one I'm eating in the picture.

But before you make the roses you'll need to ice your cake, and this is what you do:

1 Butter Icing This is just *4 oz. of margarine and 8 oz. of icing sugar* mixed together. Beat until the mixture turns almost white in colour – your wrists will ache! To make chocolate icing add *2 dessertspoonsful of chocolate powder* (or 2 oz. of melted chocolate). Add coffee powder if you prefer a coffee-flavoured cake, and by using a few drops of colouring you can turn the icing pink or green.

Put your sponge on a cake board or large plate – this will be the brim of the hat. And with a spatula or big knife, spread the icing all over the cake and the board, or plate.

2 Cover the cake and the board with a pattern made by using a fork. You can see how the finished effect looks like woven straw. When your fork gets clogged with the butter icing, wipe it clean and dip it into a bowl of hot water before starting on the next bit of the pattern. You will find you will probably have to do this quite often. You can also keep your spatula clean in the same way when icing the cake. This will give the cake a really smooth surface before you start on the pattern.

3 The Rose Mixture You can make the roses from marzipan, or the sort of mixture you use for peppermint creams – without the peppermint. This mixture is far cheaper than marzipan, and you will need: *1 lb. of icing sugar; one lightly whisked egg white; ½ teaspoonful of glycerine and some colouring.*

Mix the white of egg and the icing sugar together. Start off with a spoon and finish with your hands. Add a few drops of colouring, and also the glycerine. The glycerine is not essential, but it will stop the mixture becoming too dry.

4 Making the Roses Mould a small piece of the mixture into a triangle shape with a rounded point. The tip of the point will be the centre of your rose. Roll five smaller pieces into small balls and squash each one flat. These are the five petals. Wrap one petal round the top of the triangle, then add the others, attaching the centre of each new petal to the join of the one already on the triangle.

5 When all the petals are wrapped round the top of the triangle, cut them off with a sharp knife. (The part of the triangle that is left behind can be built up to form the foundation for your next rose.) Gently bend the tips of some of the petals to get the effect you want. You can vary the size of your roses to suit the size of your cake, and you can make rose buds, too.

6 Decorating the Hat Make as many roses as you want to put round the brim of the hat and save two or three of the best ones for the top.

I made the leaves by colouring some butter icing green and placing it on the cake with the tip of a sharp-pointed knife.

Don't worry if you spoil a few roses to start with, you can just put them back in the bowl and remould them.

Scone Pizza

QUESTION What has Princess Anne's wedding got to do with my Scone Pizza?

ANSWER I said give your Mum a rest and let her put her feet up and watch the wedding on the telly while you made my Scone Pizza for her dinner — which is what hundreds of Blue Peter viewers did! And I'm glad to say my Scone Pizza was a great success. Judging by the letters you wrote, even Fanny Cradock would have been proud of the testimonials I received!

Joking apart, it's a really simple recipe that's great for using up left-overs. I like mine hot, but the pizzas are quite tasty cold, too, which makes them useful for picnics as well as TV snacks.

These are the ingredients you will need:

For the scone mixture:
8 oz self-raising flour
2 oz fat—any hard fat will do, but don't use a soft margarine
a pinch of salt and some pepper
a little milk
a little extra fat for cooking
For the toppings I used:
onion rings—partly cooked
scraps of cooked bacon
cheese, chopped tomato,
hard-boiled egg and sardines.

After sieving the flour into a bowl, add the salt and pepper; next add the fat, rubbing it into the flour using your fingers, until the mixture looks like breadcrumbs. This takes about 30 seconds.

Begin stirring the milk in—*don't* add too much at first—and mix until you have a sticky dough which will hold its shape.
Melt some fat in the bottom of a frying pan and put the mixture in, levelling it out with a wooden spoon. Cook on a medium heat until the underside is done—about ten minutes.

Using a slice, turn the scone over and cook for about another ten minutes. (If you want to cook the scone in the oven, put the mixture into a greased baking tin and cook in a pre-heated oven—Gas Mark 8 or 450°F.—for 12 to 15 minutes or until it has risen and is a golden brown.) By the way, if you're not allowed to use a stove yet, you will need some help from an adult with the cooking. If you are using the stove remember to keep the pan handle turned away so that there is no danger of knocking it over or of any young members of the family being able to reach it.

While the scone is cooking, prepare the topping. Slice the onion into rings and pre-cook them in a little fat until they're clear but not brown. Slice the cheese, chop the cooked bacon into small pieces and cut up the tomatoes (they can be tinned ones)—or hard boil your eggs and open your tinned sardines. Arrange the topping on your Scone Pizza, making sure you leave the cheese until last.

Finish your Scone Pizza off by cooking it under a medium grill for about ten minutes *or* put it back in the hot oven, on the top shelf, for ten minutes.

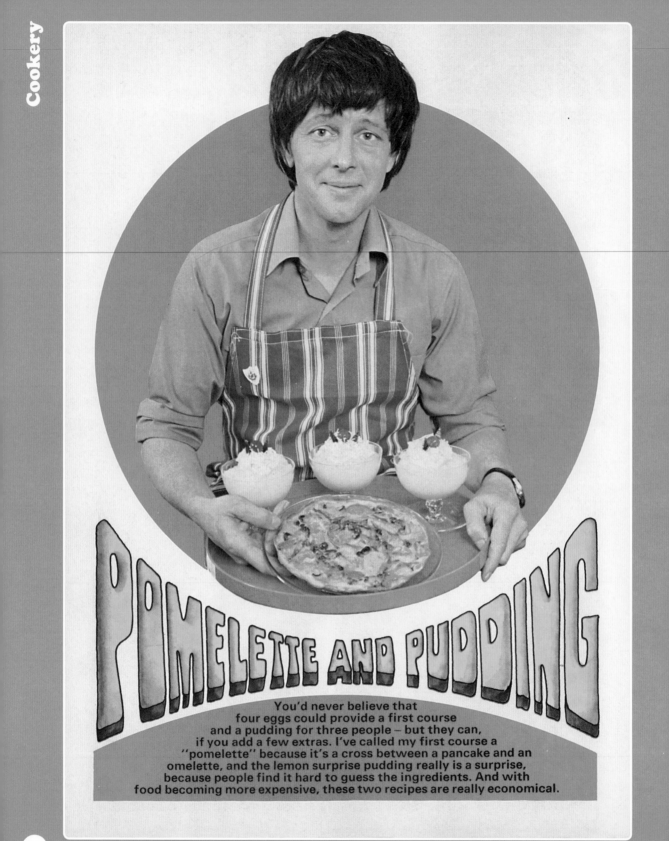

POMELETTE AND PUDDING

You'd never believe that
four eggs could provide a first course
and a pudding for three people — but they can,
if you add a few extras. I've called my first course a
"pomelette" because it's a cross between a pancake and an
omelette, and the lemon surprise pudding really is a surprise,
because people find it hard to guess the ingredients. And with
food becoming more expensive, these two recipes are really economical.

Pomelette
Ingredients
2 egg yolks, 2 whole eggs,
left-over scraps, Like bacon,
cold potatoes, ham,
cold vegetables
4 teaspoons of self-raising flour
1 tablespoon of milk
salt and pepper

Melt a little fat in a frying pan, add left-overs and cook on a low heat.

While this is cooking, whisk eggs lightly in a basin, (saving the two spare egg whites) add salt and pepper, flour, milk, and mix thoroughly.

Pour the egg mixture over the food in the frying pan and let it cook.

Then turn it over (piece by piece, don't try to toss it!)

When properly cooked, serve on a warm plate.

Lemon Surprise
Ingredients
1 packet of lemon jelly
2 egg whites - left over from the pomelette.

Make the jelly with water as directed on the packet and leave until cold, but not completely set.

Whisk 2 egg whites until stiff.

Pour jelly over egg whites

mix gently until the egg white is the colour of the jelly.

Pour into individual glasses and leave in a fridge or cold place to set.

decorate and serve.

Any flavour jelly can be used, so you could have Raspberry, Strawberry, Blackcurrant or Lime Surprise.

Take it easy with

HARD TIMES BISCUITS AND FRUITADE

Times may be hard—but even if you're down to your last few pence, you can live like a lord with my Hard Times biscuits and cheap Fruitade.

These are two recipes that are really economical. At the same time they taste delicious and would be very useful for a party or picnic.

You can make about twenty biscuits from this recipe. The fruitade recipe makes approximately a litre of concentrated juice. The citric acid acts as a preservative so the juice can be kept for up to three weeks (refrigerated). This recipe is a particularly cheap one and works out at less than 1p per glass when diluted with water.

BISCUITS

Ingredients:
5 oz. (125 g) fat
2 oz. (50 g) sugar (brown or white)
2½ oz. (65 g) porridge oats and
2½ oz. (65 g) self-raising flour
    mixed together
1 egg
Glacé cherries (optional)

Method

1 Put fat (half margarine and half lard) into a mixing bowl, and cream until smooth.

2 Beat in the sugar.

3 Add the egg (*or* two left-over yolks or whites).
4 Add the mixed oats and flour.

5 When all the ingredients have been beaten together roll the mixture into balls about the size of a walnut, then place on a *greased* baking tray.

6 Slightly flatten the tops of the biscuits, then if you like you can place half a glacé cherry on the top of each. (N.B. Remember to allow enough space between the biscuits for the mixture to spread when it's cooking).

7 Put the trays in the oven at Regulo 325°F (Gas Mark 3) and let the biscuits cook for about 10 to 15 minutes.

8 After removing the trays from the oven, lift the biscuits from the tray with a spatula, place on a wire tray to cool.

9 When cool, the biscuits are ready to eat. Store any left over in an airtight tin.

FRUITADE

Ingredients:
1 orange   1 lemon
(You could also use grapefruit—or a mixture of all three)
½ oz. (15 g) citric acid
1 lb. (500 g) sugar
1 pint (500 ml) water

Method

1 Grate the rind off the orange and the lemon and put the rind into a mixing bowl.

2 Squeeze the orange and lemon and add the juice to the rinds.
3 Add the citric acid and the sugar and stir well.

4 Boil the water in a kettle. The water must be boiling, so ask a grown-up to help you with this.
5 Carefully pour the boiling water on to the mixture then set aside to cool.

6 When cold, strain through a sieve to get rid of all the bits of rind.
7 Then bottle, and the fruitade is ready to serve, diluted with water.

BE MY VALENTINE-AND EAT IT!

You wouldn't think that three old bananas could turn into a mouth-watering cake *and* four sumptuous party trifles. But that's what happens with my New Zealand Banana Cake recipe. The basic mixture is delicious in itself. But with a bit of imagination you can transform it into a special St Valentine's cake—and nothing's wasted! The bits you trim off to make the heart shape can be used as a basis for banana trifles.
Why not send a Valentine with a difference next February 14th—an edible one.

BANANA CAKE

Ingredients:

3 bananas (old ones are best)
4 oz (113 g) butter
4 oz (113 g) sugar
6 oz (171 g) self-raising flour

2 tablespoons of milk
1 teaspoon of bicarbonate of soda
2 eggs

1 Cream together the butter and sugar.

2 Mash the bananas and mix them into the butter and sugar.

3 Beat the eggs in another bowl, then beat into the mixture.

4 Put the milk in a cup and stir in the bicarbonate of soda.

5 Mix the flour and the milk into the main mixture, about a third at a time and alternating between the two.

6 Put the mixture into a greased cake tin (a square one if you want a heart shape) and cook for 45 minutes at Gas Mark 4, or 350ºF. or 180ºC. After 45 minutes you should be able to push a skewer into the centre of the cake and pull it out with *no* mixture sticking to it. If necesary cook a little longer.

BANANA TRIFLE

The crumbs left over from trimming the cake to a heart shape can be used for individual trifles by adding custard, instant whip, or jelly, and topping with cream and slices of fresh banana.

DECORATION

For a Valentine cake, bake in a square tin and cut the heart shape like this:

Cover with butter icing (creamed butter and icing sugar) or lemon icing—icing sugar mixed with lemon juice or lemon squash. Decorate with cherries, chocolate flakes, hundreds and thousands and silver balls.

SAVE THE CRUMBS
For the trifles.

TORTILLA ESPANOLA

IF YOU FANCY GIVING YOUR FAMILY AND FRIENDS A REAL TASTE OF SPAIN THEN THIS IS THE RECIPE FOR YOU. IT'S A TRADITIONAL SPANISH OMELETTE AND YOU CAN SERVE IT FOR BREAKFAST, LUNCH OR TEA. IT'S REALLY FILLING, CAN BE EATEN HOT OR COLD, AND IS SIMPLICITY ITSELF TO MAKE.

INGREDIENTS:
2 large potatoes – peeled and diced
1 onion – chopped
1 green pepper – chopped
1 large tomato (or 2 small ones) – chopped
3 tablespoons olive oil
4 large eggs
salt and pepper to taste

Boil the potato cubes for 8 to 10 minutes, then drain. Heat 3 tablespoons of oil in a non-stick frying pan and add the potato, chopped onion, green pepper and tomato. Stir and cook slowly for about 15 minutes. Crack the eggs into a bowl and whisk. Remove the vegetables from the heat and add to the egg mixture. Stir and season. Now pour the mixture back into the frying pan, adding a little more oil if necessary. Cook for about 5 to 7 minutes, until the bottom of the tortilla is cooked and the top is still a little runny. Remove from the heat. A simple way to cook the top is to grill the tortilla for a few minutes until golden brown. Or put on oven gloves and turn the tortilla over by putting a plate over the frying pan and quickly turning it upside down on to the plate. Then slide the tortilla back into the pan to cook the other side.

Chocolate treat!

Torrone Molle is sometimes called fridge cake and is simple to make although its ingredients aren't cheap. If you have a special occasion coming up and want to create something deliciously different to impress your friends and relatives try this Italian cake. Cut it into thin slices or small squares as it's rich and crunchy and a little goes a long, long way.

Here's how you make it

Prepare a cake or loaf tin for the Torrone Molle by lining it with cling film. This will make the cake easier to remove once it is finished.

Now to the cooking proper. Place the butter and cocoa powder in a clean mixing bowl and, using a large spoon, beat them together until they are well blended, smooth and creamy. Then mix in the ground almonds. In a saucepan, dissolve the sugar in a little water over a low heat and add to the mixture. Pour in the honey, stirring really well. Finally fold in the broken biscuits before putting the mixture into the prepared tin. Press the mixture firmly into the corners of the tin and level the top with a spatula. Cover with cling film and put in the fridge for at least four hours.

Take the Torrone Molle out of the fridge, just before you're ready to serve. For an extra special occasion, decorate it with whole almonds or crystallised violets.

Here's what you need
150g unsalted butter
150g cocoa powder
150g ground almonds
150g granulated sugar
water
1 tablespoon honey
150g Petit Beurre biscuits broken into small pieces

THIS CAKE CONTAIN NUTS SO MAKE SURE THAT IT IS NOT EATEN BY ANYONE WITH AN ALLERGY TO NUTS.

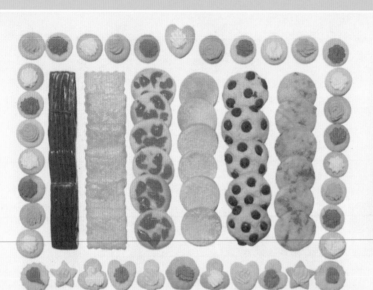

No such luxury as these for the evacuees during the Second World War – they'd have taken a whole week's ration of butter and sugar! But by 1979 standards it's an economical recipe and the results are delicious!

Use the basic recipe and add your favourite flavouring. These biscuits make good presents for Mums and Dads, Aunts, Uncles and Grandads – as well as Grannies. Put them in a decorated jar for an extra special touch.

Granny's Biscuits

Variations on Basic Recipe

Cherry, Coconut and Squashed fly Biscuits
Mix cherries, coconut or currants with flour and sugar before adding lemon and egg.

Candy Kisses
Mix a little icing sugar with some water, add a few drops of colouring, and put small dots in the middle of the biscuits.

Chocolate Chip Biscuits
Make small balls of mixture and push in chocolate chip pieces before cooking.

Basic Recipe

200g or 8oz } self-raising flour

100g or 4oz } castor sugar

100g or 4oz } butter or margarine

1 egg (beaten)

Rind and juice of half a lemon

Pinch of salt

1 Mix flour, sugar and salt in a basin. Rub in butter or margarine until the mixture resembles breadcrumbs.

2 Add grated rind and juice of half a lemon and beaten egg. Mix to a stiff paste.

3 Roll out thinly on a well-floured board. Cut into circles.

4 Place on greased baking sheet and cook in moderate oven at 160 degrees C/235 degrees F, Gas mark 3 for about 15 – 20 minutes, until pale golden.

Chocolate Finger Biscuits
Melt an ordinary bar of chocolate and spread it over biscuits (cut out in oblong shapes)

Coffee Cream Sandwich
Sandwich two biscuits together with icing made from
50 g or 2 oz butter
100 g or 4 oz icing sugar
Teaspoonful of instant coffee dissolved in a few drops of hot water.

Jars
Decorate your jars with pictures cut from cards or magazines, coloured sticky tape, or shapes cut from sticky-backed plastic or wallpaper. Paint the lids with enamel paint.

SPUD- WICHES

Here's a tasty snack for tea or supper. Spud-wiches are best eaten hot. The ingredients are all very simple—ones you're likely to have handy without doing any special shopping.

Next time you invite your friends to tea, why not try them out?

1 You will need:
1 lb. of mashed, cooked potato, 2 eggs, corned beef, or any other tinned meat, milk, tomato sauce, a teaspoon of salt and pepper.

2 Mash the potatoes finely until they are dry and flaky (a good tip is to drain the water from them after they're cooked, and return the saucepan to the stove for a few seconds, letting them "cook" without water. This will evaporate excess moisture).

3 Divide the mixture in two and flatten one half to about $\frac{1}{4}$" thick (6 mm.) Spread with tomato sauce (or horse-radish, mustard, or any favourite flavour), cover with slices of meat, about the same thickness, then more sauce and a final layer of the other half of the potato.

4 Beat the egg yolks with a little milk and pour into a shallow dish. Cut the potato sandwiches to a convenient size, dip each one into a saucer of seasoned flour, then the egg yolk and milk mixture, and finally the flour again.

5 Fry the spud-wiches in hot, shallow fat, turning them so that they brown on all sides. If you are not allowed to use a frying pan, ask a grown up to help with this stage. Serve hot with gravy, or a sauce made from tinned soup.

APPLE LAYER CAKE

Is it a cake or is it a pud? Actually, it's both!

ALL YOU NEED TO MAKE IT IS:
6 eggs • 150g sugar • 1 lemon
150g plain flour • 150g melted
butter (cool) • 2 cooking apples

Preheat the oven to 180˚C or gas mark 4.
- Separate the yolks and whites of 6 eggs and whisk the whites until they form peaks.
- Add the sugar in two halves. Beat the first half into the egg whites then use a large metal spoon to gently fold in the rest.
- Grate the yellow skin of the lemon finely.
- Beat the egg yolks with a fork then add the lemon zest. Fold the yolk mixture into the whites.
- Sift the flour and fold in a little at a time. Add the melted butter then stir everything together.
- Grease a 20 cm diameter round cake tin and dust lightly with flour. Put just less than half the mixture in the cake tin and pop it in the oven for about 10 minutes until this layer has set slightly.
- While the first layer is cooking, peel, core and slice 2 cooking apples. Take the cake tin out of the oven and carefully spread the apple slices over the first layer. Now pour on the rest of the mixture to make the final layer.

- Put the cake back in the oven for about 45 minutes. When it's ready the cake should be brown and slightly shrunk away from the sides of the tin. A handy tip for testing is to pop a skewer into the middle and if it comes out clean, the cake is done.

Leave the cake to stand for 5 minutes before turning out on to a cooling rack. Our Apple Layer Cake can be eaten hot or cold and is delicious served with custard or cream.

Blue

Everyone loves a pizza so if you're having a party or simply thinking about treats for your packed lunch box, here are some tasty ideas.

Pizza Toppings Ideas:

- sliced tomato and onion
- cheese feast (a mixture of cheeses)
- ham, mushroom and olives
- pineapple sweetcorn and tuna.
- chicken and peppers

Blue Peter

Ingredients:

- ready cooked pizza base or for small pizzas try a sliced muffin
- tomato pizza topping
- cheese (mozzarella is the real thing but any grated cheese is ok)
- dried herbs (oregano or mixed)

Whichever base you choose, spoon on a dollop of tomato pizza topping and spread it all over.

Pizzas

Sprinkle on some herbs and then start dreaming up tasty toppings. Sliced fresh tomato, onion and cheese is always a winner. Or how about a cheese feast if you have a few varieties in the fridge? Ham and mushroom is a good combination as is tuna and sweetcorn.

Put muffin pizzas on a baking tray under a medium grill until the cheese starts to bubble – this takes around 5 minutes. If you are using a ready-made pizza base, follow the instructions on the packet.

Pizzas can be enjoyed piping hot or cold.

Blue Peter

ANTHEA TURNER
Blue Peter presenter 1992-1994

Since a child I have always loved arts and crafts. My Dad comes from an artistic family, mainly in woodwork, and my Mum was always making things with me and my sisters. In fact, I was awarded my first *Blue Peter* badge at the age of seven when I sent in an idea of how to make a mouse out of shells that I'd collected on a beach in Tenby, South Wales. It took me 25 years to get my next badge when I joined the team as a presenter in 1992, and it didn't take long for me to put my hand up to every *Blue Peter* 'make' I possibly could. Luckily for me my fellow presenters, John Leslie, Diane-Louise Jordan and Tim Vincent, were only too happy to pass.

I loved and relished all my makes but the one that stands out above all the rest was making Tracy Island. The company who produced the toys for *Thunderbirds* had vastly underestimated the popularity of their plastic model of Tracy Island. Shops were running out and children were disappointed. The Editor at the time, Lewis Bronze, stepped in and said, 'Don't worry, we'll make one.' Easier said than done! Margaret Parnell was drafted in out of retirement (she had created many iconic *Blue Peter* makes) and was the woman for the job. After a week she came back with what is probably the most famous make in *Blue Peter* history. What you see on the live television show is a very slick operation but to get there took hours of preparation, patience and practice. Everything had to be exact and timed down to the last second. I can't tell you how many practice ones I made and 'Here's One I Made Earlier' stages, but I think to this day in my sleep, I could still make you a model of Tracy Island. The one I made on the show was given to me when I left. I wouldn't part with it for the world, because not only is it a little piece of *Blue Peter* history it's mine and captures a moment of great personal pride.

Here's One
I Made Earlier

Toys & Games

DOLLS FOR YOU TO MAKE

Valerie will show you how

Do you like Cinderella and her sisters or the gay Dutch doll? Their clothes are scraps from the rag bag, but can you guess what the dolls themselves are made of? Turn to the next page and Valerie will tell you.

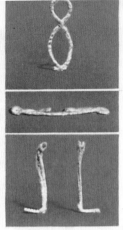

Did you guess that the dolls are made from pipe cleaners? All you need to make a doll of your own are four pipe cleaners, some pink or white wool, some material for the face and a little cotton wool

Use one pipe cleaner for the head and body. One for the arms. One for each of the legs.

Join them together by folding over the tops of the arms and legs on to the body.

Now cover the doll with wool. Any thickness will do, but a fine wool makes a smoother finish.

Head Pad with cotton wool, cover with material and sew down the back very tightly.

Face Embroider the eyes, nose and mouth with a fine thread, and make the hair out of loops of wool.

Arms Begin at the top and wind the wool evenly down. You add more and more layers until the arms are thick enough. Oversew the hands with a needleful of wool.

Body Pad with cotton wool and cover with a layer of wool.

Legs Make in the same way as the arms.

Shoes Embroider them in silk or wool.

Now the dolls are ready to dress in any way you wish.

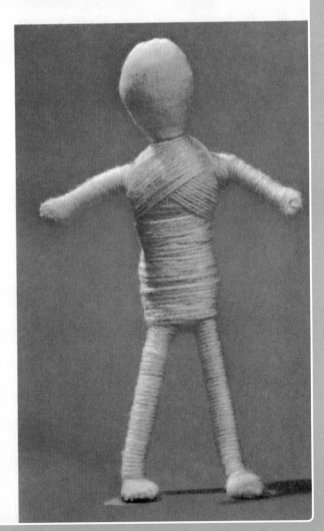

TEDDY

The pride of the Regiment

Teddy is all ready to go on parade.
His uniform is made from squares and oblongs of
plain knitting. It is very easy to make, and if you are
going to knit one you will need:

Pair of knitting needles
Red, black and navy wool, and an oddment of
yellow for the strap
Elastic for the trousers
Piece of red ribbon
Brass paper fasteners
White tape and small buckle

And this is how you make it,

The Tunic

1 *Back:* In red wool cast on enough stitches to fit half way round Teddy's waist. Knit until it is long enough to reach from the shoulder to an inch or so below his waist.

2 *Fronts:* Cast on half the amount of stitches used for the back and add two or three extra to allow for overlapping. Knit until it is the same length as the back. Make another piece exactly the same.

3 *Sleeves:* Knit a piece wide enough to reach from wrist to shoulder, and long enough to go round the arm quite loosely.

This is how you sew the pieces up

4 Join the two front pieces to the back at the shoulders. Next sew on the sleeves at the shoulders. Then sew all along the sleeve seam and down the side of the tunic. Now change to navy wool for the collar and the trousers.

5 *Collar:* In navy wool cast on enough stitches to go round Teddy's neck. Knit about four rows and cast off. Knit two small pieces in navy for the shoulder tabs. Sew in place and fix on shoulders with a brass paper fastener.

6 **Trousers:** In navy wool knit two pieces each long enough to reach from the waist to ankle, and wide enough to go half way round his waist.

7 Join each section about half way up, and then join both pieces together to form trousers. Sew a piece of red ribbon up each side, and thread elastic through the top.

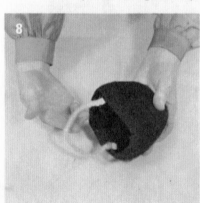

8 **Bearskin:** In black wool knit an oblong wide enough to fit comfortably round Teddy's head and the height required. Sew up the short sides, and sew across the four corners to shape the top. Turn right side out and brush with a wire brush to make fluffy. Plait some yellow wool to make the strap, and sew in place.

9 For the finishing touches, put the tunic on and do it up with brass paper fasteners for buttons. Add a belt made from white tape and a little buckle, and Teddy will be all ready to mount guard.

Pyjama clown

Do you remember when Valerie made this Clown Pyjama Case? You can make him out of scraps, but if you haven't got the right bits you can buy everything you need for about 3s.6d.

Fold an oblong of material into a square big enough to hold your pyjamas or night dress.

Fold the material with the right sides together and sew along the three open sides.

Cut a slit across the back—**not right to the points**—and turn right side out. Be careful to cut *only* the back.

Blanket stitch along the edge of the slit to stop the material from fraying. You can do this in any colour you like. If you use plain material, you may like to have different coloured stitching.

Make paper patterns of the face, hands and feet and draw on to thin plastic foam. You will need two faces, four hands and two feet. If you prefer, you can cut the feet out of coloured felt.

Cut out eyes, nose and mouth from coloured felt and sew on to one of the foam faces. Sew round the edges of the hands, head and feet, but leave the bottom open so that you can join them on to the body.

Stuff the face with cotton wool using enough to make it round and fat. Stuff the hands and feet in the same way.

Poke one corner of the body into the neck and pin in place. Poke one corner into each hand and the bottom corner into the feet. Sew into place.

Trim round neck and hands with a frill. Start with a piece of ribbon. Sew along one edge, pull the thread at one end: the ribbon will gather into a ruffle.

Make a pointed hat from a triangle of material and sew along the seam.

Finish off with woolly pom-pom. When you put them on, make sure the seam is at the back.

Make two pom-poms for buttons, and fasten the back slit with poppers.

PETE AND POLLY

If you're always forgetting to clean your teeth, Pete and Polly might remind you – they're toothbrush holders and they're made from plastic bottles and plastic foam.

Only *part* of the plastic bottle is needed. After painting it and letting it dry, cut away the piece marked here with black stripes.

Stick the top to the bottom section with sticky tape. Don't worry if the join looks untidy as it will be covered by the 'hair'.

When Pete and Polly have been decorated they're ready for their toothbrushes. Their hats are made from circles of plastic foam with a hole in the middle.

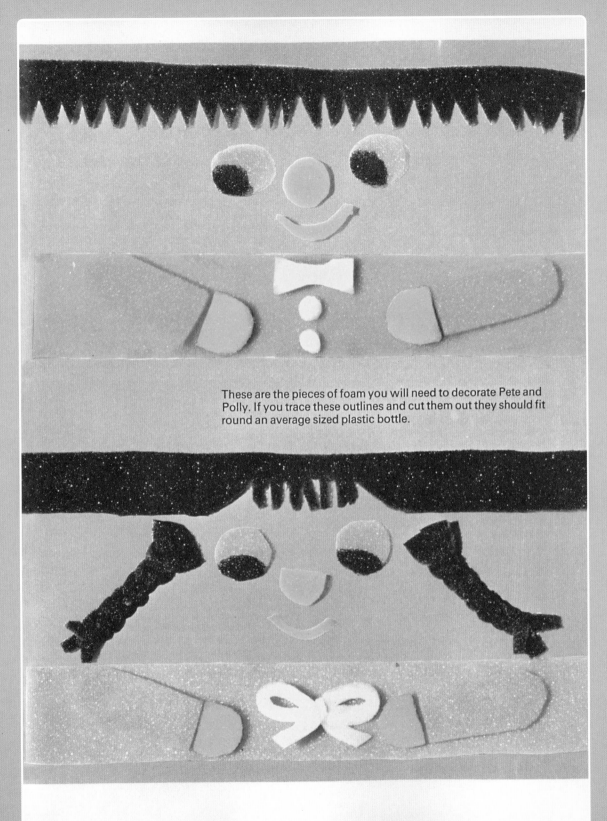

These are the pieces of foam you will need to decorate Pete and Polly. If you trace these outlines and cut them out they should fit round an average sized plastic bottle.

Would you like to have a flying wing? From one polystyrene tile you can make two gliders like mine for a few pence. Launched by a really strong, thick elastic band, they'll stay aloft for ages and perform all sorts of aerobatics.

FLYING

First of all, find the centre of a polystyrene ceiling tile. Draw two lines from corner to corner of the tile. The point where they cross will be the exact centre.

Starting from the centre point, measure off three inches along each line and make a mark. Join these marks together and you will have an exact square in the centre of the tile.

WING

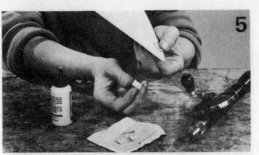

Cut the tile in half along one of the lines you have marked from corner to corner. Each half will make a glider. Next, cut away the small triangle and you have the basic flying wing shape left.

To weight the nose, use two pieces of one-sixteenth inch plywood, half an inch square. Drill a hole through each piece. Glue one piece of plywood to the top surface of the wing, near the nose. Push a three-quarter inch nail through the hole in the plywood and through the wing. Glue the other piece of wood and press on to the nail from the underside of the plane.

For final trimming, bend up the trailing edges of each wing and slightly bend up the wing from the centre. Catapult by hooking a large elastic band to the nail.

Using a medium sandpaper, smooth along the top of the wing so that it tapers from the leading edge at the front of the tile to the trailing edge at the back. Finish off with a smooth sandpaper. Do not taper in the centre near the nose, as this is the place to hold while catapulting.

All these gliders are made from polystyrene tiles – and all of them fly. After you've tried the flying wing, see what planes you can design.

SHOE BOX HOUSE

Here is an idea for a doll's house you can make for yourself. Because I had six boxes it has got six rooms, but you can make yours any size you like. It all depends how many boxes you have got. And if your doll's house family gets bigger it is easy to add another floor.

1 Mark windows on five of the boxes. I cut a window in a box lid and used it for a pattern. Using a pattern makes it easy to get all the windows the same size.

2 Mark the front door on one box and cut carefully round three sides. Score down the fourth side to make a hinge so that the door opens easily. Fasten with a door knob made from a paper fastener.

3 Glue the boxes firmly together.

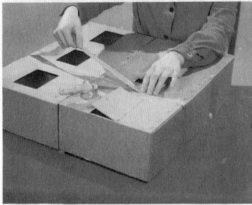

4 Strengthen the joins with sticky brown paper. When the house is painted the strips will not show.

5 You will need four box lids to make the roof. Cut away one long side and one short side from each lid. Slot them together two at a time and glue firmly.

6 Place the roof on the house and cover with corrugated card to give a tiled effect. Cut shutters from corrugated card and glue in place at each window. The house is now ready for painting.

7 Paint carefully over the front of the house in a good strong colour. This will hide the sticky paper joins. A chimney made from a small box and two corks is a good finishing touch.

8 Paint inside the house as well and furnish with your doll's-house furniture. In my house I've cut a fitted carpet for the bedroom from a piece of felt and at each window I've glued scraps of material for the curtains.

TABLE TOP TANKS

Do you collect models of vintage vehicles? Here are some you can make for yourself. These are Mark IV tanks. They took part in the first major tank battle at Cambrai, in France, over fifty years ago. To make them, all you will need is cardboard, matchboxes and glue.

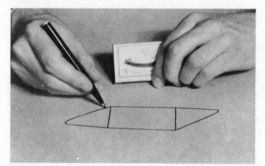

1 Start with the sides. Lay a large matchbox on a sheet of thin card and draw round it. Make a mark about two inches from each end of the box shape and draw in the curve for the front and back of the tank.

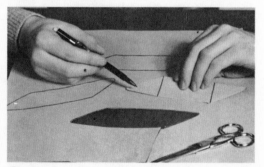

2 You will need four pieces of card exactly the same size. Cut out your first shape just inside the outline and use it as a pattern.

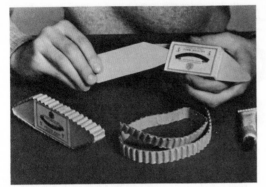

3 For each side slot two pieces of card through a large matchbox. Glue on a strip of corrugated card to make the caterpillar tracks.

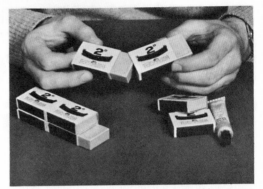

4 You will need four small matchboxes to make the body of the tank. Cardboard ones are best. Take two of the boxes, push the trays out about $\frac{1}{2}$ inch, and slot them together. This makes the fuel tank. Two more boxes glued together and stuck on top complete the body.

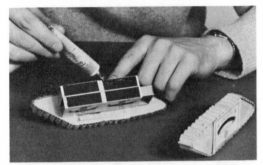

5 Glue the sides to the body. Remember to keep the body clear of the tracks and to put the fuel tank at the back.

6 Both side gun turrets are made from one large matchbox tray. Mark the tray as I have done. First cut the box in half then trim away the angles. Fill in the open side with a little piece of card.

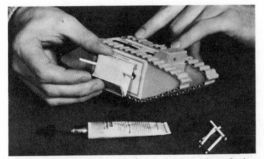

7 Stick one gun turret on each side of the Mark IV and add guns made from used matches. The top turret is made from half a small matchbox tray.

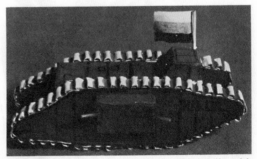

8 Paint the Mark IV green and add details with a black pen. I have made Hilda, the famous tank that led the battle of Cambrai. You can make a layout with a tray of earth or sand and some twigs.

Witches & Wizards

Can you turn someone into a toad? Can you cast spells? I'd be very surprised if you could! But here's a bit of magic anyone can work. Make a few magic passes over a dish-mop and a plastic lemon and you can transform them into a witch or a wizard. If you'd like to make special weird glove puppets, here's what to do:

1 To make a witch's head, first cut the screw top off a plastic lemon. The pointed end will be the nose. Next, cut two holes, one at each side, just big enough to take the handle of a dish-mop.

2 Push the dish-mop handle right through the holes in the lemon and arrange the strands like straggly hair. If the mop hair is too thick, give your witch a haircut.

3 An easy way to make the face is to cut the eyes and mouth from black sticky-backed plastic. If you make the corners of the mouth turn down, your witch will look nice and nasty! If you want to paint the features instead, it's easiest to use enamel paint as this will stay on the plastic lemon best.

4 Fold an oblong of material in half and draw a witch's dress on it. Felt is a good choice as it won't fray when you cut it out. Make a tiny hole at the neck to push the dish-mop through. The dress should be long enough to hide the dish-mop handle and big enough for you to wear as a glove with one finger in one sleeve, and your thumb in the other. Sew or stick the side seams together and turn the dress the right side out.

5 To make the witch's hands, cut four mitten shapes from a different-coloured material. Sew or stick them together in pairs, but before you close the wrists, push a little stuffing inside to fatten them up. Then sew or stick the hands firmly into the witch's sleeves.

6 The stiff black paper hat is made in two pieces. First cut a fan shape, fold it into a cone, and glue down the edge. Next cut a circle for the brim. A cottage cheese carton lid makes a good pattern. Then cut a smaller circle inside, snip round the inside edge and bend up into little tabs. Glue the tabs inside the cone and decorate the finished hat with silver paper stars.

7 For a finishing touch, I've made my witch a cloak from an oblong of material. Put a hem down one long side, thread a piece of tape through, gather up the material and tie it round the witch's neck. You can glue on silver stars and moons to make it look witch-like. I've made her a broomstick, too, from a little bunch of twigs tied to a stick.

8 You can make a wizard in just the same way. When I trimmed his dish-mop hair, I saved the pieces to glue under his nose for a moustache and beard. Wizards' hats don't have brims, so I've glued the cone-shape straight on his head.
Use one hand to make your witch's arms wave and use the other to hold the dish-mop handle which makes her head nod. With a little practice you can make her cast spells!

Freight Train

COAL TRUCK

1 Cut a piece of thin card the same length as the truck and a little wider. Bend the sides to make a little platform which will slot neatly into the truck.

2 Crumble a piece of a polystyrene ceiling tile into granules. Cover the top of the card with rubber solution glue and stick on the granules.

3 When the glue is dry, paint the granules with black poster paint to look like coal.

Make your railway pay by running fully loaded goods trains. Container wagons are expensive, so get empty trucks and fill them yourself with home-made freight. It's a cheap and easy way to add realism to your layout. Here's the freight I've made to be carried by the 532 Blue Peter.

STONE CHIPPINGS

Make a little cardboard platform to fit your wagon in exactly the same way as for the coal truck. This time glue on lentils to cover the top and paint them grey to look like stone.

SHORT PIPES

1 Using your truck as a pattern, cut a piece of card to fit the floor.

2 Glue bits of macaroni to the card in neat rows. Paint them grey or brown to look like drain-pipes.

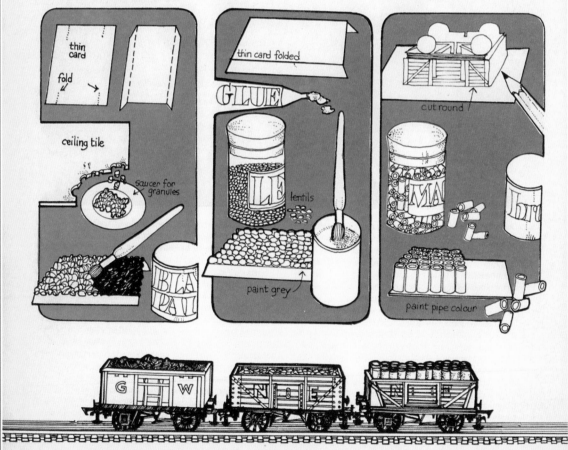

LONG PIPES

Drinking-straws cut in half make good drain-pipes. Glue the first layer to a piece of thin card, then glue more straws on top to make a full load. When the glue's dry, paint the straws a "pipe" colour.

TIMBER LOAD

Save up ice-lolly sticks and convert them into planks. Trim off the rounded ends and split each stick down the middle to make two planks from each one.

LOG WAGON

Cut garden twigs to the same length as your wagon and to stop them rolling off, glue them to a piece of card. A bit of chain from a broken necklace glued over each end of the twigs is a good finishing touch.

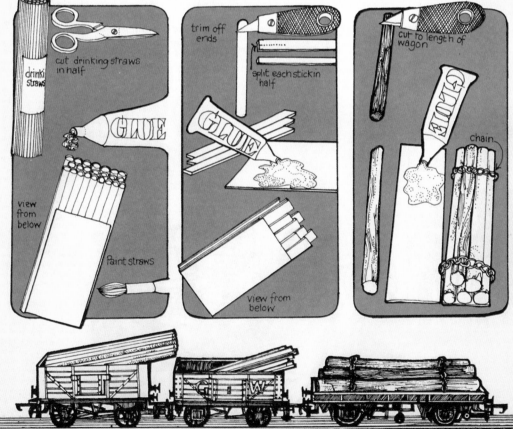

MARBLE CASTLE

From a grocery carton, some cardboard tubes and some egg boxes, you can make a game that all the family can play. It's cheap and it's fun, and if you make it carefully, it should last for ages. Here's what to do.

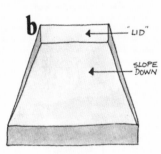

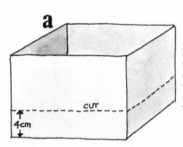

1 THE BASE

a) Mark a line about 4 cms from the bottom of a grocery carton and cut carefully. When you've finished it will look like a lid.

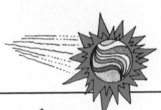

b) From one of the left-over sides, cut a piece of card the same size as the "lid". Glue it in place to make a slope. One short side should fit into the bottom of the "lid" and the other should rest on the edge. It's down this slope that the marbles will run.

c) To make the game more fun, you'll need some obstacles. Make these from egg boxes. Cut out the egg sections and, using just a dab of glue, put them roughly in place. Roll a marble down the slope to make sure it will hit the obstacles and not run straight through. When you're satisfied, glue the egg sections firmly in place. Don't make the run too easy!
Paint the finished base all over with emulsion paint. For extra strength, a top coat of gloss is a good idea.

2 THE TOWERS

a) Make towers from cardboard tubes from kitchen towel or toilet rolls. You'll need four about 4 cms high, and one a bit taller. In each one, cut an arch for a marble to get through. Paint the towers, and when they're dry, draw in the stonework with a black felt-tipped pen.

b) Glue the small towers in a row at the bottom of the slope. Cut the bottom of the tall tower at an angle to match the slope and glue in place at the top.

3 FLAGS & RULES

Cut out scoring flags from paper or sticky-backed plastic stuck on to cocktail or match sticks and glue in place at the top of the small towers.

To play the game, drop a marble down the big tower and try to get it into a scoring tower. Add up the points as you go along. In our rules,

the winner is the one who gets the most points in six throws, but you can make up your own. Hope you enjoy it. We do!

Box Farm

If you would like a farm-house to complete your farm set, here's an idea for making one from two shoe boxes. There's a real door that opens, see-through windows made from cellophane, a porch made from a shallow box, and for a finishing touch, I've thatched the roof with raffia.

1 It's easiest to make the porch and doorway first. Draw a door shape on a small cardboard box or box lid, and cut along three sides. Leave one long side uncut so that the door can be opened.

2 Put the porch on one side of a shoe box and draw round it. Next, cut out the card about half an inch inside the lines you've drawn and bend the card that's left outwards along the lines.

3 Draw in the windows and cut them out. It's a good idea to cut a piece of card for a pattern so that all the windows will be the same size. Glue the porch firmly in place and leave it to dry.

4 Next, paint the house. I've used emulsion paint, but any un-shiny paint will do. When the paint's dry, stick pieces of cellophane inside the box to make the windows. If you cut the cellophane bigger than you need, it's easier to stick in place, and the extra bit won't be seen from the outside. I've used strips of sticky plastic for the panes and matchsticks for the frames.

5 To make the front door look real, cover the front with wood-grained plastic or coloured paper. Then push a brass paper fastener through to make a door knob. Make a roof for the porch from a little piece of card with strips of raffia glued on to make the thatch. Glue it into place.

6 For the roof, use a second shoe box. Cut down in a sloping line from the corners and then cut along the bottom of the box and you will have a roof shape that fits the house. Thatch the roof with raffia, or real straw if you can get it. Paint the sides of the roof to match the house.

7 Make a chimney from a piece of a cardboard box that toothpaste has been packed in. All you have to do is cut a V-shape in each side so that it fits on to the roof. Paint the chimney, and when it's dry, mark in the bricks with a black pen or pencil.

8 If you've got two more smaller boxes, you could make a little cottage to go with the farm. The boxes don't have to be the same size as each other, but here's a useful tip. Keep the biggest box for the roof, or your cottage won't look right!

Explorer's Kit

Mountaineering and arctic exploring need special equipment. Here are some ideas for things to make for your soldier doll to help him survive an arctic winter. There's a sledge, an ice-axe, snow goggles, and a climbing rope – and all of them can be made from scraps.

 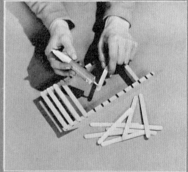

1 The Sledge For the frame you will need two lengths of wood about 10 inches long and ½ an inch wide, and two more pieces a bit shorter than a lolly stick. The two long pieces are the runners, so saw off the front ends to make them slope. Sandpaper all the wood smooth.

2 Fix the runners apart with the two smaller pieces of wood. You can stick them with impact adhesive, or you could use panel-pins for a really strong job. The slats on the sledge are lolly sticks or balsa strip. You will need about 13 slats and it's a good idea to mark their positions on the frame before sticking them in place.

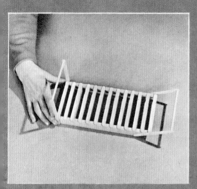 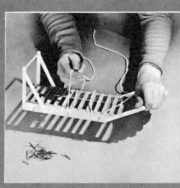

3 Both ends of the sledge are made in the same way. Cut a piece of $\frac{1}{4}$-inch dowel the same length as a lolly stick. Glue or panel-pin a stick to each end of the dowel. Glue the front end along the slope of the runners and the back end upright.

4 For extra strength for the back upright, stick two more lolly sticks from the top sloping down to the runners. Then knock two or three panel-pins halfway into the side of the runners and bend them down into hooks. These are to hold the rope.

5 Rope the supplies in place with a piece of white string. Paint matchboxes to take your explorer's supplies, make bedding rolls from scraps of materials, and cover all the equipment with a small piece of plastic to keep it snow-proof.

6 The Equipment The climbing rope is a coil of white string. Cut the shape of the axe from a plastic bottle and cover it with silver paper. Make a tiny hole in the axe and push it down onto the handle, which is a manicure stick. To make the goggles, cut two rings from the top part of a plastic soap bottle where the soap comes out. Fix them together with fuse wire and tie on some thin elastic to go round your explorer's head. Glue the goggles firmly onto a piece of coloured cellophane. When the glue is dry, cut away the spare cellophane.

GARDEN GLAMOUR

Let your doll relax in a luxury swing hammock in her own beautiful garden. A shoe-box and two wire coat-hangers can be converted into a comfortable seat, and with some ceiling tiles you can make lawns, rose beds and even an ornamental pond.

1 The frame for the swing hammock is made from two stiff wire coat-hangers. Cut the hooks off and straighten the wire outwards into the frame shape.
Keep the little curved bits at the end because they make good feet. By winding white sticky tape round the frame you can fasten the two hangers together and give them a smart finish at the same time.

2 The seat is made from a shoe-box. Cut one side off at a slope, then paint it, or cover it with sticky-backed plastic.
Thread two pieces of white string through little holes in the box and fasten them with a knot. This makes the white ropes for the seat to swing on.
When you're satisfied that the seat is hanging straight and even, fasten the ropes in place on the frame with a little piece of sticky tape.

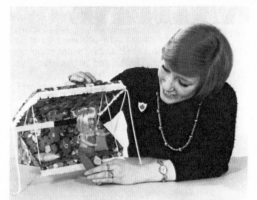

3 Cover the shoe-box lid to match the seat and make a shady canopy.
Cut two slots about a third of the way along the short sides of the box so that it will slip over the top bar of the frame. Then fasten it firmly to the bar with sticky tape.

4 White fringe trimming glued round the seat and the canopy gives the swing hammock a very glamorous look.
You can make little cushions from scraps of material, too, so that your doll can lie back in luxury and enjoy her garden.

5 Patterned ceiling tiles are ideal for the garden because, painted with grey emulsion or poster paint, they look just like crazy paving. The separate pieces cut out easily too, so you can use them to make rockeries or walls.
For grass you can paint the plain side of the tile green, or cover them with green material if you happen to have some.

6 With three tiles you can make a pond with real water. Take the middle out of two tiles and make a smaller hole in the top tile. Glue all three together with the one with the small hole on top. Make sure to use a white glue—other kinds dissolve the polystyrene. Paint the surround grey, and then slip a small plate or saucer underneath to hold the water.

7 For a realistic look, glue the spare pieces round the pond to make a little rockery wall. It's easy to make plants, too, by folding coloured paper tissue into flower shapes. When they're glued on to cocktail sticks, or spent matches, they can be "planted" straight into the ceiling tiles.

8 With the left-over pieces of tile, all sorts of things can be made for the garden. Little bits of foam plastic stuck on to real twigs make good trees. These can be planted in plasticine, pressed into a piece of tile with a wall round to give a nice finish. I wonder what ideas you'll have for your garden?

THUNDERBIRDS
ARE GO!

It was a hit TV show in the 1960s and it was a summer smash movie in 2004. So if you'd like to create your very own Tracy Island you will need the following:

- Large grocery carton
- Sandpaper
- Cereal packet for cardboard
- 2 medium and 1 small matchbox
- Newspapers
- Foam Sponge
- Kitchen foil
- Drinking straw
- PVA glue
- Corrugated cardboard
- Soap powder packet
- Brass paper fastener
- Oblong cheese box

- Pipe cleaners
- Paper bowl
- Green, brown and blue paper
- 2 washing-up liquid bottles
- Matt paint in green, brown and grey
- Small adhesive labels
- Sawdust
- 75mm flower pot saucer
- Sticky tape

Blue Peter

Base

Using the side of a strong grocery carton, draw a rough rectangular shape (about 35cm x 50cm) with three rounded corners and the fourth jutting out to allow for Thunderbird 2's runway. Cut it out.

Thunderbird 2 Hangar

Cut away the flaps at one end of a soap powder packet. Cut away the other end at a sloping angle so that it will fit the back of the base facing the runway. Fix the packet to the base with strips of sticky tape. The building on top of the hangar is a cream cheese box painted grey. Fix just the back edge of this box to the hangar with sticky tape overlapping the hangar front by about 3cm. The box should not be fixed at the front, as the hangar door will slide under it later. Keep the cheese box lid to use as part of the house at a later stage. Use part of a paper bowl for the curved roof. To get the right shape first cut off the outer rim then cut the remaining piece in half. Paint grey. Secure the corners of the roof to the sides of the building with sticky tape.

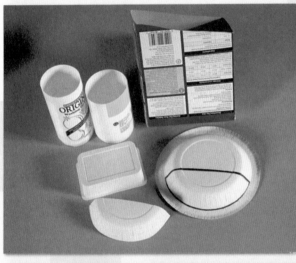

Thunderbird 1 and 3 Launch Pads

These are made from washing-up liquid bottles. For Thunderbird 1 cut the bottle down to about 12cm in height. Fix to the middle of the base with sticky tape. Cut the bottle for Thunderbird 3 to about 14cm in height. Fix to base near remaining front corner with sticky tape.

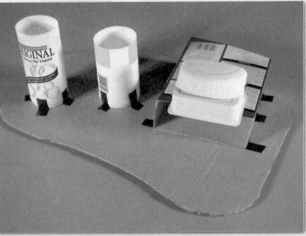

Blue Peter

The Landscape

The shape of the island is built up from crumpled newspaper spread with PVA glue. Thin the glue down with water to make it go further, then brush the glue on a half sheet of newspaper. Crumple the paper then press it onto the base with more glue. Don't use too much – just enough to hold the paper in place. Leave spaces for a beach at the front and a small cave at the back. Build up the landscape to the height of the tub in the middle and leave a few centimetres below the top of the second tub uncovered. The areas around the tubs should be fairly flat, as should the space at the

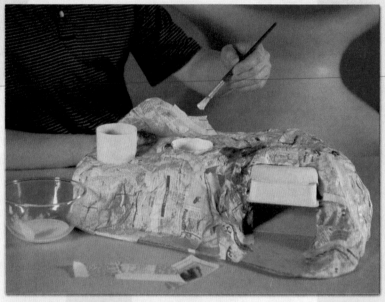

back where the house will be placed. Completely cover the soap powder packet except for the ends. Pile up paper over the building and roof and some more at the back for hills.

Finish off by gluing on strips of paper overlapping each other to hold the whole thing together. Leave the base somewhere warm to dry. The base should feel quite light when it is dry. You could make the house and trees whilst waiting for the base.

Blue Peter

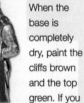

When the base is completely dry, paint the cliffs brown and the top green. If you add some sawdust to the green paint it will give a grassy look. Paint the outside of the Thunderbird 3 launch pad tub grey. When all the painted parts are dry, glue a piece of sandpaper on the beach area and inside the bottom of the cave.

6 The windows on Thunderbird 2's runway building are blue self-adhesive labels. You could easily colour white ones. Cut the labels off in a strip to fit the front of the building, leave on the backing and glue them in place.

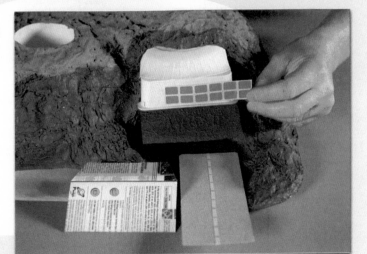

7 The hangar door is a rectangle of cereal packet cardboard covered in kitchen foil. Paint it brown to match the cliffs. It should fit the hangar front with an extra flap that can be bent over at the top and then pushed into the space between the hangar and the building – the door can then slide up and down when Thunderbird 2 is ready to launch.

Thunderbird 2 Runway

8 Cut out a rectangle of stiff card and paint it grey. Make markings down the centre from strips cut from sticky labels. Glue the runway onto the base in front of the hangar.

Swimming Pool

9 Cut out a piece of cereal packet that will fit over the centre tube and overlap it all round. Cut a hole in the middle to allow Thunderbird 1 to lift off. Cut out a rim for the pool a little larger than the opening, cover both pieces with kitchen foil to give texture and then paint them grey. When the paint is dry, glue a piece of blue card or paper under the rim. Fix the two layers together with a small brass paper fastener. This will allow the swimming pool to slide to one side for lift off. Glue the pool in place over the centre tub. Stuff the bottom of the tub with paper so that the tip of Thunderbird 1 is just beneath pool level.

Blue Peter

Observation Tower above Thunderbird 3 Launch Pad

Cut out another piece of cereal packet to fit over the tub, cover with foil and paint grey to match the swimming pool surround. The circular building at the top is made from a flower pot saucer.

Cut a hole in the bottom the size of the tub opening. Glue the top edge of the saucer to a ring of card that also has the tub-sized hole cut out of it. Paint grey, fix on blue labels for windows then fit it over the tub edge. Stuff with paper so that Thunderbird 3 shows just above the tower top.

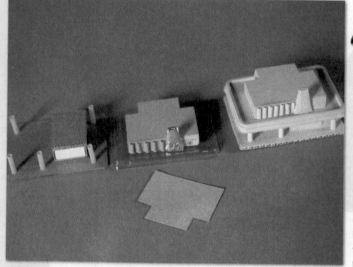

The House

The main building on the upper storey is made from a medium sized matchbox with a section from a second box taped at the back. Make a chimney from two layers of thick card, cover with foil for texture, then glue to the long side of the complete matchbox. Glue a strip of corrugated cardboard by the side of the chimney. Cover the tops of the boxes with a piece of card to cover the join. Glue the buildings to the lid from the cheese box.

The lower floor of this building is a small matchbox with some layers of cardboard glued on to make it higher. Glue onto a base made from a piece of thick card the same size as the cheese box lid. Paint the two sections grey then glue them on top of each other with pieces of drinking straw in between them for pillars. Fix the house on the flat area behind the swimming pool.

Steps

Cut a small strip of corrugated card to form steps between the house and the swimming pool and another to link the observation tower to the pool. Paint the steps grey and glue in position.

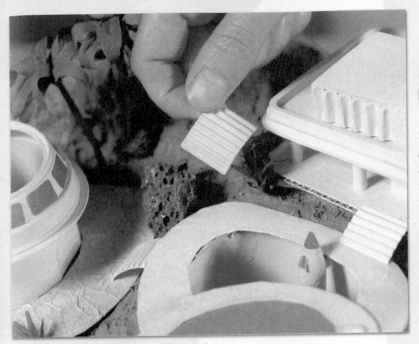

Trees and Bushes

The palm tree trunks are pipe cleaners cut in half with brown paper wrapped around them. Cut out strips of green paper and shape into leaves

and glue around the top of the trunks. Spread out the tips of the leaves so they look realistic. Make small holes with the tip of a pencil at each side of the runway then push the end of the tree trunks into them. The trees disguise the runway and can be pushed aside for launching Thunderbird 2. Fix more trees on the green area of the island. Make a few bunches of leaves for plants and some bushes from scraps of foam sponge coloured green. When fixed in place they can be very useful for covering up any torn or bare parts.

This is the most popular make in the history of Blue Peter!
We hope you'll enjoy making it

Blue Peter

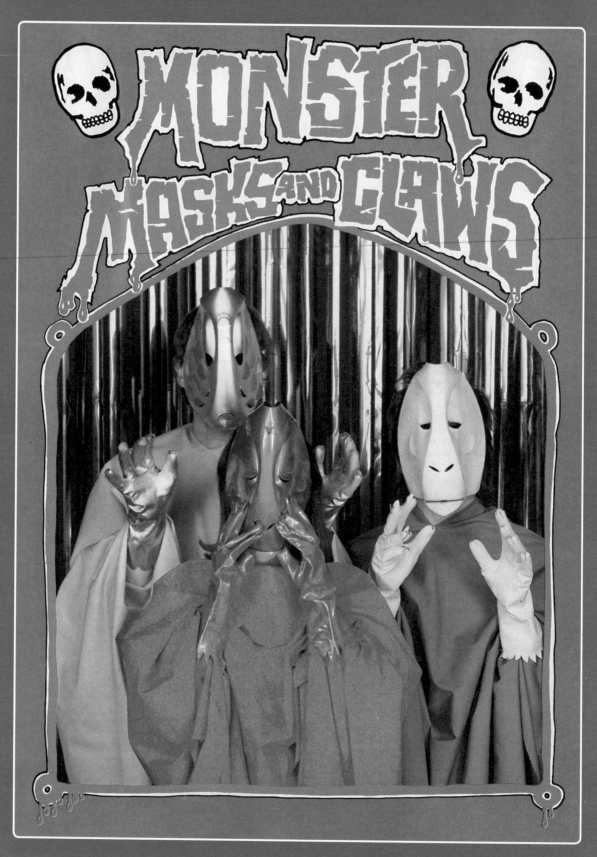

MONSTER MASKS AND CLAWS

GO WILD

at home and terrify your family and friends with your own monster masks! They come with matching claws – no horror show is complete without them!

For each Monster you will need a
2 litre size fabric conditioner bottle (with built-in handle)
Squash bottle top (for eyelid pattern)

Fine sandpaper
Paint and elastic (optional)
Old rubber gloves

1 Remove the cap of the fabric conditioner, soak the bottle in water until the label peels off, and rinse and dry the bottle thoroughly.

Cut off the top of the bottle around the rim where the cap edge fitted.

2 Using small scissors, cut straight down the join line farthest from the handle. The plastic may be thicker and harder to cut towards the bottom of the bottle – to avoid this, cut diagonally out to the corners.

Important: If it's hard getting the scissors into the plastic, make a hole with a screwdriver or bradawl – then push in the point of the scissors. Always take your time and cut out very carefully!

Claws for monster hands and feet

Using old rubber gloves, cut the finger tips and wrist edges into points, and paint them to match the mask.

Some paints don't dry on rubber, so check by painting one of the pieces you have cut away from the wrist edge.

3 Cut halfway along either side of the base of the bottle. Bend the flap over the outside of the uncut part of the base to form the lips and mouth of the mask – the pointed part can be trimmed to shape later.

Bend flap over to form lips and mouth of mask.

4 Open up the mask and draw in the cutting lines for the eyes – one either side of the handle. (We used the cap from a squash bottle to draw round as a pattern for the eyes.) Draw halfway round the cap so that the semi circles face down towards the mouth. Neatly cut along the lines you have drawn.

5 Bend up the flaps to form the eyelids and check that you can see out of the slits. If you can't, cut them a little bigger. Cut out as many slits and holes as you like to give your mask its own special character, but it's a good idea to draw on your design first, **before** you cut it out. Trim all the cut edges as neatly as possible and smooth them down with fine sandpaper so there are no sharp edges or points.

You can leave your mask plain, or if you prefer, you can paint it. For a wrinkled effect, glue a layer of torn-up tissue on the surface, using wallpaper paste. When the tissue is thoroughly dry, cover it with emulsion or undercoat paint.

You may find that the mask will grip your head firmly enough to stay in place. If it doesn't, make a hole at the back on each side and thread some elastic through, tying a knot at each end on the inside.

Use a paper fastener, with the head-end inside, to keep the mouth of the mask folded up shut.

Willo the Wisp

I'll never forget the day the Blue Peter studio was taken over by Willo & Co. Kenneth Williams, who invented all the voices, kept me and the whole of the camera crew in fits as he became Arthur, the cockney caterpillar, ratty old Evil Edna the witch who casts spells with her indoor aerial, and Mavis Cruet – the overweight fairy.

Nick Spargo, the artist who dreamed up Willo the Wisp, says there are between 2500 and 3000 different drawings in every film, so you can imagine how long it takes to make each one. But you'll find you can whip up your very own Arthur and Evil Edna quicker than Edna could turn you into a frog!

Materials needed to make Arthur

30 cm square of tan felt
Sewing thread to match tan felt
Scraps of coloured felt
Felt-tipped pens or crayons for features
Rubber solution glue
Stuffing (cotton wool or tissue)
Wire, two lengths of 40 cm and 15 cm
Round button or bead for nose
Table tennis ball
Black paper or thin card

For Evil Edna

Dark grey and light grey paper
Scraps of yellow, white and blue paper
Small buttons (3)
A small cardboard grocery packet
A black felt-tipped pen
A domed tap washer and wire

Arthur

1 Arthur's head is made from a table tennis ball. His nose is a round bead or button. Take a piece of wire about 40 cm long and bend in half, then thread the bead along to the middle and twist the ends together. To attach the nose to the head, make two holes in the table tennis ball as shown (get an adult to help with this). Thread the wire through the centre hole and out through the second hole.

His eyes and cheeks are made from scraps of coloured paper, or felt glued into position. His mouth is drawn in felt tipped pen, practice first with pencil.

2 Arthur's hat is made from a strip of tan felt measuring about 13 by 4 cm.

Fold the felt in half and in matching thread, sew the two ends together about half way down. Then in similar running stitches, sew all the way round the long edge and leave the threads long.

Pull the threads together to gather the felt into a hat shape, then firmly oversew the end and turn the right side out.

Pull

When glued on Arthur's head, the wire fits through this gap.

3 Arthur's "appendages" are petal shaped pieces cut out of the tan felt (9 pieces in all will be needed).

Sew 5 of these petal shaped appendages together in a bunch, then glue them to the top of Arthur's hat.

Then glue 2 more petal-shaped pieces under Arthur's chin.

~ **wire**

4 Arthur's body is made up in sections. Cut out small circles of the tan felt and sew all round the edge in small running stitches (leave the ends of the thread long).

—7 cm—

Pull the threads to gather into a pouch and then with cotton wool or tissue as stuffing, shape into a small cushion. Oversew the end very firmly and fasten off.

Squash the pouch into a flatter shape and then with a bradawl or pointed scissors make a hole right through the middle of the section. With the gathered side down, thread the section onto the wire and push up to the head.

arms **loop**

5 Arthur's arms are a length of the wire about 15 cm long and looped in the middle. The hands are shapes cut from black paper or card

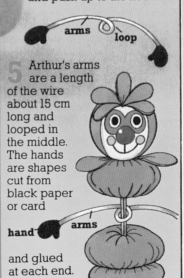

hand **arms**

and glued at each end.

Thread the arms into position and then continue making body sections as before.

Thread 8 more of these onto the wire and then twist the spare wire at the end into a flat loop. This can be hidden under the gathered edge of the last section.

Make one final cushion but do not make a hole in it. Glue the gathered side of this, to the last section on the wire to complete Arthur's body.

petal shaped appendages

wire hidden under here

Bend Arthur to shape, so that he sits up properly. You may need to experiment a little to get the balance right.

Arthur is now very nearly finished.

Add the finishing touch by sewing the last 2 petal shapes of tan coloured felt together, and then gluing them to the top end of the last body section, as shown here.

Arthur is now complete.

Evil Edna

1 Evil Edna is made from an old grocery packet, something like a suet box will do. The one that we used measured 11.5 x 8.5 cm.

Begin by covering the box neatly, all over in dark grey paper. Take care not to get glue on the outside of the covered box.

grey paper

2 Next in the light grey paper cut out the TV screen. (Ours measured 9 x 7.5 cm). Round off the corners neatly to give the correct shape. Before you stick this into position it is much easier to first complete the detail on Edna's face.

Draw carefully in pencil first and then when you have got the expression just right, draw in black felt pen. Complete the finer details with yellow and white paper for the eyes and teeth.

When Edna's face is complete, (make sure the ink is dry so it does not smudge) carefully glue it into position leaving space for the control knobs.

3 The aerial is very simply a piece of wire pushed into a domed tap washer and bent into shape as below.

Then carefully glue the completed aerial to the top of the box, as below.

aerial

domed tap washer

grocery packet

coloured paper glued to leg

Use the glue sparingly and avoid spilling excess glue on the model.

4 The 3 large control knobs are buttons covered with discs of the dark grey coloured paper. Use the buttons as a pattern to draw round, then cut out the grey paper circles and glue them on to the buttons.

paper disc glued to button

The smaller control knobs are simply cut out of the light grey paper and glued into position below the other knobs.

5 Evil Edna's legs are made from narrow strips of strong cardboard (we used the corrugated kind) glued together to make a double thickness. For the legs cut 4 lengths about 5 cm long.

Then make 4 shorter lengths about 3.5 cm long for Edna's feet.

Glue the foot on to one end of the leg piece and open out the other end a little way.

Finally cover the sides of the feet and legs with strips of blue and white paper.

leg

foot

DRESSING UP

WHETHER you're dressing up for a play or a fancy dress parade, or simply want to try out a new hairstyle, a wig like these could transform your appearance. Ready-made wigs can be expensive, but you can go punk, dizzy blonde, or bright ginger for only a few pence – and even Goldie found Simon hard to recognise!

THE BASE for all the wigs is a plastic mesh fruit or vegetable bag. (The larger the mesh, the easier it is to thread the wool or string through). The bag should be big enough to fix over your head and cover your face a little way down. Don't worry if it comes down too far because the spare bit can be tucked up inside the wig.

Woolly wigs

1 Try to use a thick, chunky type of wool, (If you're using a thinner wool, use two strands at a time.) Cut off 10-12 cm lengths – not all exactly even. The wig looks better if it's slightly shaggy and uneven.

— 10cm —

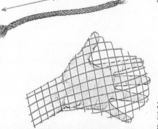

2 Put one hand inside the bag fairly near the top and spread out the mesh. Thread a strand of wool in one hole and out of the next and tie the ends of the wool over the knobbly part where the mesh is joined. Continue to tie on the strands, working evenly downwards to cover all the mesh.

3 Try the wig on when you think it's big enough. If it is, just tuck up the spare mesh inside and it's ready to wear. You can vary the effect by using different types of wool. Simon's blonde wig is wool that has a ready-made curly effect, but you can get much the same look by using unpicked wool. Cut the strands longer than for straight wool, and you don't need to tie on so many pieces as the length covers up the gaps.

LUNA PEDES

Our Galactic Lunapedes may not be as big as Paul Jefferies' radio-controlled caterpillar, but they're lovely movers, and they're a lot less complicated! The more you practise manipulating their strings, the more you can make them do and you don't have to build Space scenery for them – they're lots of fun on their own. And in the true Blue Peter tradition – they don't cost an arm and a leg to make – all you'll need is an old ping-pong ball, some buttons and beads, a cotton reel and some old lolly sticks.

1   For the Lunapede's head, make two eyeholes in a table-tennis ball just above the join line – about 2-3cm apart.

Use a bradawl to make the holes, but take great care – you may need an adult to help with this bit. Enlarge the holes with a small pair of nail-scissors.

2   Make a hole for the neck on the opposite side of the ball from the eyes, and a fourth hole in the top of the ball for the antennae.

3   A good tip for painting the head is to push a straw or stick into one of the holes to keep the ping-pong ball steady while you paint it. We used silver paint – but any colour will do. Stand the straw in a jar while the paint dries.

DO NOT OPEN HATCH IN ORBIT

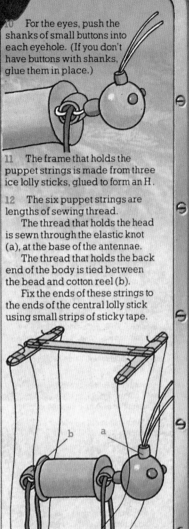

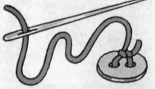

4   Paint the various parts of the Lunapede's body before you fix them together (they don't have to be exact copies of these!)

5   Thread a 30-cm length of wool through a needle and down through one hole of a large button to the underside, then up through the other hole, leaving enough wool at the end to tie a couple of knots to secure the button in place.

Thread the wool through a large bead and then fix the second large button to the end of the strand in the same way as before. Trim off the spare ends of wool. Make a second pair of legs to match.

6   Use a 50-cm length of thin elastic or string to hold the body sections together.

Push an end of the elastic through the large bead on one of the pairs of legs.

Take both ends of the elastic together and push them through the cotton reel.

7   Push one end of the elastic through the large bead on the second pair of legs, and push the other end of elastic through the bead in the opposite direction. Pull the ends of elastic tight so that all the body sections are held close together.

8   Thread both ends of the elastic through a medium-sized bead and then through a bodkin.

Push the bodkin into the neck hole of the head and out through the hole at the top.

9   Finally, thread the two ends of elastic through the last bead and pull them up tight. Tie the ends together firmly and make several knots so that the elastic will not slip through.

Trim the ends of elastic to the same length and separate them for antennae.

10   For the eyes, push the shanks of small buttons into each eyehole. (If you don't have buttons with shanks, glue them in place.)

11   The frame that holds the puppet strings is made from three ice lolly sticks, glued to form an H.

12   The six puppet strings are lengths of sewing thread.

The thread that holds the head is sewn through the elastic knot (a), at the base of the antennae.

The thread that holds the back end of the body is tied between the bead and cotton reel (b).

Fix the ends of these strings to the ends of the central lolly stick using small strips of sticky tape.

For the feet strings, sew threads through the knots that hold the buttons in place. Fix the other end of these threads to the ends of the other lolly sticks, using sticky tape.

Leave the ends of the threads loose so that they can be pulled under the tape to adjust the length.

PS   If the strings get badly tangled you can simply peel off the sticky tape, untangle the threads and re-fix them!

EE·AYE·ADDIO·WE WON THE CUP!

How's your dribbling, shooting and passing? Play your own Cup Final at home with our table football game.

Kick off:
1 large grocery carton (approx. 60 x 35 cm)
2 soap powder packets
Thin dowelling or garden canes
22 spring-clip clothes pegs

Paint or sticky-backed plastic to cover box
Green and white stiff paper or paint
Gloss paint in colours of favourite teams
Stiff card for scoring discs and

football figures
Numbers from old calendar
2 brass paper fasteners
Clear adhesive glue
Sticky tape
Table tennis ball to play game

First half:
Cut down a large grocery carton to make a shallow, open box with sides about 10 cm all round.

10cm

Make 2 goal boxes from the lower part of soap powder packets. For goal mouth cut away one long side as shown.

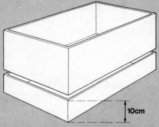

SOAP

7cm

1cm

Place goal box against end of "field" making sure it's central, then draw round it. Remove the box and draw a second line 1 cm inside the first. Cut round this second line on three sides leaving a fold-down flap. Glue goal box onto flap and side of "field".

GLUE

Stand a clothes peg against the side of "field" and mark the level of the peg hole. Make another mark 1 cm above. Do this at the other end of the box and draw a line joining the top marks together. Mark 8 evenly spaced holes along this line – make holes and test to see if they are large enough to take dowelling rods. Do this on both sides of the "field". The rods should turn easily.

Use sticky tape to strengthen all the edges, then cover everything apart from the playing field with either paint or sticky-backed plastic.

Cut a thin frame from white card to outline the goalmouth and glue into place – or use white paint.

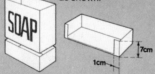

Paint the field green, or cut stiff green paper to fit the base. If using paper, cut out the base for goal boxes separately, leaving an overlap to tuck under the main sheet of paper. Glue these goal mouth pieces into place. Before glueing the main sheet mark the goal areas and centre line in white card or paint. Glue firmly in place.

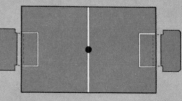

Half-time
If using paint, have a half-time rest and let it dry.

Second half:
To stop ball becoming stuck in the corners, cut four pieces of stiff green card about 7 cm square. Fold diagonally in half to make a triangle shape. Glue one in each corner.

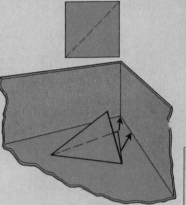

Cut rods to size. They must be 25 cm longer than the width of the box. Smooth the ends with sand paper.

Cut out a pattern to make football figures, making sure it fits the size of pegs. Draw round pattern to make 44 figures from stiff card. Cut out and paint in your favourite team's colours. Glue the figures on each side of the 22 pegs.

If you want a simpler version, you can just paint the pegs –10 in one colour and 10 in another, with 2 pegs painted green.

Slip the rods into place with equal amounts of rod on both sides of the box. Clip the pegs into place. (If any peg touches the ground, trim with sand paper.) When players are accurately in position, glue into place. Wind sticky tape round and round the ends of the rods to stop them pulling through the holes, and paint these ends to match the players on the rod.

Cut two scoring discs from stiff white card. Paint numbers – or cut out figures from an old calendar and glue round edge of disc. Attach to side of box with a brass paper fastener, positioning discs so that they overlap the corner of box to make turning easier.

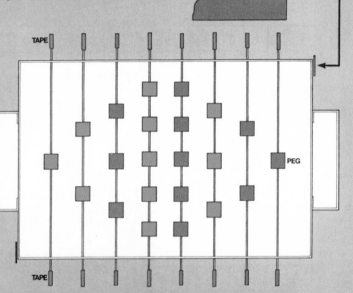

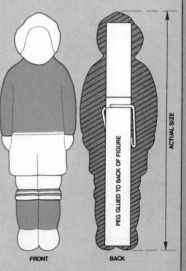

FRONT   BACK

PEG GLUED TO BACK OF FIGURE

ACTUAL SIZE

TAPE

TAPE

PEG

Full time:
Find another football fan. Toss a coin to see who throws the ball in and kick off! Get together a few of your friends, form your own league and have your own cup matches. Now you can have your own *Match of the Day* any time you like!

Make
Edd the Duck
Olympic Superstar!

Edd's the British team's mascot for the Barcelona Olympics. Help him cheer on our team by making your own Edd glove puppet, dressed in an Olympic-style jogging suit. Awesome!

You will need
A yellow foam sponge ball
Yellow wool
Bright green wool (for his hair)
Kitchen-roll tube
Old white vest or T-shirt fabric
Orange and yellow felt
Glue

The head

1. Use the marking on the ball to make a downward sloping slit – that will be Edd's mouth. You can do it by snipping carefully along the line with scissors. Taking that as a guide, make another slit where his hair will go. Below the mouth, cut out a hole about the size of a 10p piece.

2. Wind the yellow wool around four fingers about 10 times. Carefully cut through the loops to make strands. Snip off pieces 0.5 cm long.

3. Spread a little glue at a time on the head and press plenty of fluff on. Cover the head.

4. Fold 10-cm bundles of the green wool in half. Glue them into the hair slit.

5. Stick the orange and yellow pieces of felt together. The pieces should be about the size of a large biscuit, with the yellow piece slightly larger. Fold the felt so the yellow is on the outside. Stick it into the mouth slit in the head.

6. Edd's eyes are small oval pieces of white paper. Use a black felt-tip to draw in the pupils. Draw them looking down.

The jogging suit

1. Cut an oblong of the white material, 14 cm × 24 cm, and fold it in half. Cut a small semi-circle out of the folded end – that's for the neck.

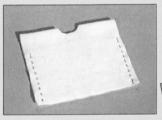

2. Sew or glue the sides up, leaving small holes at the top for Edd's hands.

3. Cut mitt shapes out of yellow felt. Each hand is two shapes glued together. Leave the wrist ends open so your fingers can fit in.

4. Sew or glue the hands into the open ends of the jogging suit. Fold in the bottom of the jogging suit and sew or glue it.

5. The trousers are two more strips of material – same width, but half the length. Cut a slit in the middle, and fold the edges over into a V-shape. Glue or sew into position.

6. The feet are made the same way as the hands. But you don't leave a gap when you glue them into the bottom of the jogging-suit trousers.

7. The neck is a centimetre-wide strip of cardboard tube from a kitchen roll. Glue or sew the neck into the collar of the jogging suit. Glue the head on top, making sure that the hole you made in the sponge ball is over the neck hole.

awesome

JANET ELLIS
Blue Peter presenter 1983-1987

It takes a certain sort of person to look at a margarine tub and think, 'Doll's bath'. Or to be asked to create a Dr Who Monster Mask and rush straight to the cleaning cupboard for a plastic bottle. Luckily, for many years, *Blue Peter* had just such a person on hand. Margaret Parnell was a one-woman powerhouse of ingenuity. Not only that, but she invested the 'makes' with two vital things – access to ingredients and simplicity of execution. There's no point in showing the young viewer something so complicated that they lose interest by stage 2 or in using items that require a trip to a specialist shop. We *might* have been guilty of asking people to empty the washing up liquid container before its time, but at least it was already on the shelf.

I loved the 'makes'. I'd been pretty handy at crafts myself, as a child. And as a presenter, it was six glorious minutes in the programme's busy running order when I knew I'd remember my script. The saintly Miss Parnell sent each 'make' in its composite parts (and several versions, for rehearsal), so that there was no danger of wondering what came next. Bliss!

I don't have a favourite 'make', but anything with glitter always got my vote (still does). I'm not sure if my daughter Sophie has ever forgiven Margaret and me for having to model the snood, though.

Here's One
I Made Earlier

Christmas

An Advent Crown for Christmas

Just like the villagers of Oberndorf all those years ago, people in Britain decorate their homes at Christmas time and, of course, we always decorate our 'Blue Peter' Studio.

But there's one decoration that goes up before all the others – and that's the Advent Crown. The idea is that it helps you to look forward to Christmas – rather like those calendars where you open small doors and windows until you reach Christmas Day itself. The Advent Crown has four candles. The first one is lit on the first Sunday in Advent. On the second Sunday you light the second candle and relight the first. On the third Sunday you light three candles, and on the fourth Sunday you light all four. The four candles are lit again on Christmas Eve if it happens to be a weekday, although this year the fourth Sunday in Advent **is** Christmas Eve.

If you've watched 'Blue Peter' at Christmas time you'll know that we always make our Advent Crown ourselves, and this is a good idea, because it's a large decoration, and one that would be very expensive to buy.

These are the things we use: fireproof tinsel and ribbon, coloured glass balls, thin wire, plasticine, some tin lids, and some wire coat hangers. The frame work of the Crown is made in two halves, and for each half you will need two wire coat hangers. For the top half cut the hook off one of the hangers and wire them in position so that they form a cross.

The candle holders are made by fixing a small lid on to each of the four corners. We use the lids from salad cream or chutney jars. Pierce a hole in the middle of the lid and in the side. Wire it to the hanger leaving one end of the wire sticking up through the middle of the lid.

Wind fireproof tinsel round and round the whole of the frame, including the candle holders, and fix the ends of the tinsel with fuse wire so that they do not unravel. You can use red, green, blue, silver, or multicoloured tinsel instead of gold, but it *must* be fireproof. Cover the bottom of the lids with shiny gold paper.

To fix the candles in the holders, spike them on to the wire in the middle of each lid and secure them by filling the edges of the lids with plasticine. Make sure they are so firm that they do not wobble.

The bottom half of the frame is made just like the top half, but without the candle holders. After covering it with tinsel, fix it to the top half with wire (with the hook end pointing downwards).

Decorate with the fireproof ribbon and the coloured glass balls. People find it hard to believe that such a splendid decoration started off as four wire coat hangers!

Sugar snowmen and pink mice

Here's an idea for decorating your table when you have a party – and they're decorations you can eat as well! Both the snowmen and the mice are made from the same basic mixture of icing sugar and white of egg.

This is what you do:

1 To 1 lb of icing sugar add the white of an egg.

2 Stir the mixture well until it's stiff and almost crumbly.

3 Mould a small lump of the mixture for the head and a larger lump for the body and press together.

4 Decorate with a liquorice allsort and chocolate penny for the hat – liquorice for the eyes, nose, scarf and buttons, and a glacé cherry for the mouth.

To make the pink sugar mice

1 Add a few drops of pink cochineal to the icing sugar and white of egg.

2 Stir well until all the mixture is pink.

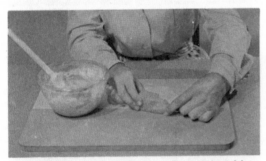

3 Mould into mouse shapes. Remember this will not work unless your mixture is really stiff.

4 Decorate your mouse with silver balls for the eyes, peanuts for the ears, and liquorice for the tail.

Miniature gardens

If you haven't got a garden of your own you could make miniature gardens to keep indoors. You can use real twigs and flowers or plastic ones that last for ever. I've made two kinds — one for summer and one as a Christmas decoration

1 The base of my garden is a round cake board. A good size is one about 8 inches across. Paint it with brown poster paint to look like earth and glue a handbag mirror in the middle for the pool.

2 Press a lump of modelling clay on to the board by the mirror. If you're not using real plants you can make a tree by wiring small plastic leaves onto a twig. Push the stem of the twig firmly into the clay.

3 When the trees are in place you can hide the modelling clay with some biggish stones.

4 You can make the grass from moss. If you can't get real moss you can get dry moss from a shop. Put some glue on the board and fix the moss in small clumps until it is covered.

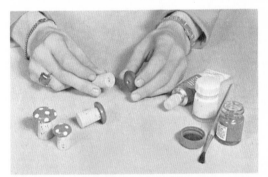

5 I've put some big toadstools in my garden. They're made from buttons glued on to corks. Paint the buttons in bright colours and leave the corks plain.

6 The small plastic flowers are pushed into little blobs of clay and pressed on to the board. Add one or two animal ornaments or toys and your garden is finished.

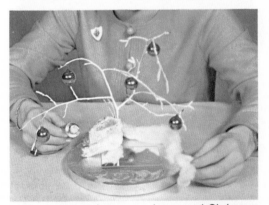

7 A snowy garden can make a good Christmas decoration. Leave the cake board silver and use cotton wool instead of moss. Paint the trees white and hang tiny decorations on them.

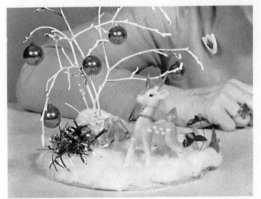

8 I've finished my Christmas garden with plenty of glitter, a little reindeer, and some holly from the Christmas cake.

TINSEL SWEET TREES

These sparkling Christmas trees are special ones because you can eat all the decorations! They are sweets wrapped in bright cellophane. When you've eaten all the decorations you can save the trees and refill them next year with fresh sweets.

To make my big tree I used: 12 inch length $\frac{1}{4}$ inch dowelling; a yogurt tub; cellulose filler; coloured cellophane; aluminium foil; gold foil paper; cardboard; tinsel; sticky tape; glue; sweets; and this is how I did it.

1 The trunk of the tree is a piece of dowelling. Fill a yogurt or cream tub three-quarters full with cellulose filler. If you haven't any filler, use modelling clay. Push the stick into the filler and leave to set firm:

2 Next cover the tub with gold foil paper and then with a layer of red cellophane. A little glue will hold the cellophane in place. Make sure that you have washed the tub well.

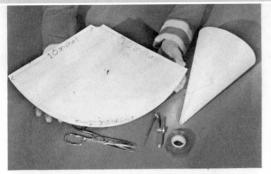

3 The cone shape of the tree is made from thin cardboard. A compass helps to get the correct shape which looks like an open fan. Cut a small piece from the top point. Bend the cardboard round into the cone shape and secure with sticky tape.

4 Cut a piece of foil paper the same shape as the cone but slightly bigger. Cover the cone with this paper. There is no need to glue the foil in place. Just wrap the foil round the cone and tuck the ends in firmly top and bottom.

5 I used about ¾ lb. boiled sweets to cover this tree, but if you use smaller sweets you may need a few more. To make shiny decorations cover the sweets with a layer of aluminium foil and then with coloured cellophane. Twist the ends into a 'tail'.

6 Cut 'X' shaped slits in the cone about half an inch from the bottom and about two inches apart. Push 'tails' of sweets into slits. Carry on round and up the cone putting in less sweets with each round. Finish off with a sweet pushed in the top hole.

7 Fix a strand of tinsel inside the cone with sticky tape. Wind the tinsel below the first row of sweets, then up round the lines of sweets to the top. A dab of glue will stop it unwinding again.

8 You can make a tiny version of the tree using small sweets wrapped in clear cellophane. A cotton reel makes a tub and a pencil a trunk. Little sweets get eaten fast, so make sure you have plenty handy to refill your tree!

A Christmas Welcome

A decorated door looks specially
welcoming at Christmas-time, so
if you're making decorations, why
not hang one outside for everyone
to see?

My decoration is made from a
polystyrene ceiling tile, a string of
tinsel, a cake doyley, some pieces
of ribbon and a bit of holly. It's
cheap and quick to make, and if
you pack it away carefully, it will
last for years. Here's how to
make it:

1 First of all, fix a string of gold tinsel right round the ceiling tile. Start at one corner by pushing a pin first through the tinsel and then firmly into the side of the tile. One pin at each corner is quite sufficient to hold the tinsel firmly in place.

2 Glue a gold cake doyley to the centre of the tile. Some types of glue melt polystyrene, so it's a good idea to check your glue first by putting a dab at the back of the tile. I found that rubber solution glue was very good. It doesn't spoil the tile, and if you make a mistake, it's easy to rub off and start again.

3 I used holly sprays to finish off the centre of the decoration. Mine's plastic, but if you can get real holly, it looks even better. Push the stems right through the ceiling tile and bend them flat at the back. A few strips of sticky tape will hold them neatly in place.

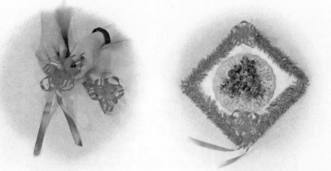

4 Make two bows, one for the top and one for the bottom of the decoration. I've used red gift ribbon, the kind that sticks to itself when moistened. Just make a loop, and where the strips meet, moisten and press together. On one bow, I've left two long ends as they look good hanging down the door.

5 For the finishing touches, pin or glue the small bow to the top corner and the big bow to the bottom, and add some small coloured balls. To hang the decoration, thread a loop of thin wire through the top point of the tile

Christmas Magic

If you said you were going to transform a newspaper into a Christmas tree, your friends wouldn't believe you! But it can be done. Follow these instructions and you'll end up with an enormous, sparkling decoration.

1 Start by spreading four double sheets of newspaper out flat. Then make a giant set of compasses by tying one end of a piece of string to a pencil and fastening the other at the top corner with a drawing pin. Gradually move the pencil and mark a curve.

2 Cut out along the curve and paste the four shapes exactly on top of one another. You can use wallpaper paste, or mix up your own from flour and water. Leave the shapes until they're dry.

3 When the paste is dry the newspaper shape will be quite stiff. Bend it into a cone to make the Christmas tree shape and fasten the edge with sticky tape. It's easier to make the cone if you snip the pointed tip off first.

4 To make the tree green, you can either paint it or cover it with a sheet of green crepe paper like I have. You'll need a packet of green tissue paper too. To make the leaves cut each sheet into 10-cm. (4") squares.

5 Pinch up the centre of a tissue paper square and twist round several times so that the four points stick up. Put a dab of glue on the twisted bit and stick the leaf on the tree. It's best to start at the top and stick the leaves quite close together so that your tree is well covered.

6 When all the leaves are dry you can wind a string of tinsel round and fasten the ends with sticky tape or a dab of glue. I'm decorating my tree with home-made stars made from gift ribbon. A pin put straight through the star and into the tree will hold it in place. You can use real decorations too — but never use candles or electric lights or your paper tree might catch fire!

7 To make the Christmas tree tub, fill a large flower pot or metal waste-paper basket, or any container you can find with earth or sand. Then push a broom handle or a thick stick firmly into the filling. You can make the container look Christmassy by decorating it with silver cooking foil, and finishing off with a ribbon bow.

8 You can make a tree any size you like just by altering the length of string on the giant compass. Shorten the string and you can make a little tree for the table; lengthen it and stick two double sheets of newspaper together before you make the curve, and you could make a tree as big as yourself!

FLOUR CANDLES

Yes! I do mean flour! There's nothing wrong with my spelling. These flower candle holders ARE flour—baked hard as nails and painted. You can make any flower you like, but I chose holly to decorate a Christmas table.

Here's the recipe:
  4 dessertspoons of plain flour
  1 dessertspoon of salt
  2 dessertspoons of water
Mix it all together into a dough and you're ready to start. This is what to do:

LEAVES

Flatten out the dough on a floured board and cut it into rough leaf shapes. I got nine out of my lump, which left a couple of spares in case of accidents!

When the leaves are cold, paint them with shiny green enamel and leave them to dry. A good tip when you paint the berries shiny red is to stick them into a lump of plasticine.

Using the tip of a spoon, nip out the holly "prickles" and mark the leaf veins on with the point of a knife. Keep all the left-over bits of dough and roll into holly berries.

LINE WITH PLASTICINE TO HOLD CANDLE FIRMLY

METAL TOP COVERED WITH FOIL AND GLUED TO BASE

CARD COVERED WITH GOLD FOIL

THE BASE

While the paint dries, make the base. Using a round lid as a pattern, cut out a circle of card. Glue on shiny foil to cover the card and fold and stick down the edges to neaten them. Cover a metal bottle top with foil and glue it into the centre. Make sure it is *metal*. Plastic could melt or even catch fire—so don't use it.

Push the berries on to each end of a bit of fuse wire and put them together with the leaves on a baking tray. Cook for several hours at a low temperature until hard and dry. If you can, put them in when a casserole stew is being cooked. That's ideal—and saves fuel, too! Look at them from time to time, and if they're puffing up, poke them flat again with a spoon. Gently, mind!

Arrange the leaves round the candle holder and glue them into place. You can either leave the berries on the wire stalks and twist them into the leaves—or take them off and glue them straight on to the base. Either looks nice, so it's up to you!

Do you remember these Father Christmas decorations? Pete and I made the big one to deliver the family presents in his sack, the middle one to bring the cards, and the little one to hold the crackers in the middle of the party table. They're all made the same way. Here's how to do it:

GETTING READY FOR CHRISTMAS

1 For a middle-sized Father Christmas, like we're making, start by pasting four double sheets of newspaper in layers and finish off with a sheet of brown paper. If you're going to make a giant Father Christmas, make another piece this size and sticky-tape the two together. Leave the paper until it dries hard.

2 The body is a cone shape, so you'll need to mark a curve. We made a giant-sized set of compasses like Val did when she made a Christmas tree. Tie a string to a pencil and drawing-pin the other end to the corner of the paper. Move the pencil gently in case the drawing-pin comes out. Cut out along the mark.

3 Fold the paper into a cone shape and fasten it firmly with sticky tape or glue. This job's easier with two people—one to hold and one to stick! Snip the top off the cone, because this is where the head and neck will slot in.

4 Now cover the body with red crêpe paper. Tuck the paper neatly down the neck and round the bottom edge and glue on the inside for a neat finish. Don't worry about the join because this will get hidden in a minute.

5 It's cotton-wool trimming that hides the join. Stick some round the neck and the bottom of the red cloak, too.

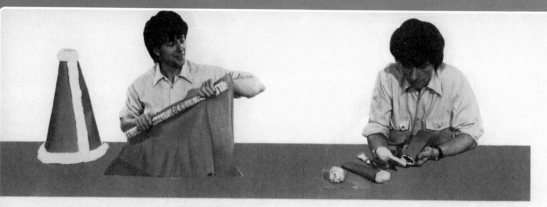

6 The arms are made from a tube of newspaper. Roll a whole double sheet up with a layer of red crêpe paper on the outside. One tube will be enough for both arms.

7 Twist some newspaper into a ball to make the hands. Cover them with pink crêpe paper and slip them into the arms with a dab of glue to keep them firmly in place. Glue the arms into place by the fur collar.

8 Next get a big ball of newspaper ready to make the head. Wind sticky tape round the neck to stop it coming apart.

9 Cover the head with a sheet of crêpe paper. For the nose, we stuck on a ping-pong ball painted pink. The eyes are black sticky-backed plastic, but buttons or black paint would be just as good. Stick on some cotton-wool hair.

10 Father Christmas's beard is a triangle of cotton wool stuck straight under his nose! That's why we didn't bother giving him a mouth! His hat is made from a cone of red crêpe paper trimmed with cotton-wool fur.

We gave our Father Christmases belts and buckles for a finishing touch—a paper one for Big, and real ones for Middle and Little. We made sacks, too, out of an old piece of material, but strong brown paper bags work just as well. We didn't give Little a sack. He's got a bunch of crackers instead, tied to his arm with a string of tinsel. Our Father Christmases looked great in the ''Blue Peter'' studio. They'd look just as good in your house, too, and if you pack them away carefully when the holidays are over, you can bring them out year after year.

Orange Delight

Orange Delight

You don't eat it—you smell it!
It's an Elizabethan Pomander and it's very
easy to make. All you need is a small, firm
orange, the cheapest cloves you can get from a
chemist, a bit of talcum powder, a paper bag
and some patience! Follow these instructions
and you'll end up with a present for a lady that not
only looks good, but smells delicious! Why not try it?

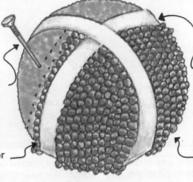

1 Use a nail or knitting needle to make holes through the orange skin. Don't put them too close.

2 Divide the orange in quarters with cotton tape. Hold in place with a pin.

3 Start by pushing the cloves in along the line of the tape. Then, for a nice finish, try to fill the space with neat rows.

4 Fill in the holes with cloves. The orange will shrink when it dries, so the cloves will end up close together.

Put the clove-covered orange in a paper bag (plastic won't do) and shake some talcum powder in with it. The cheapest unscented kind is best. Put the bag in a warm, dry place, like the airing cupboard. LEAVE FOR SIX WEEKS. When you open the bag, you'll find the orange is smaller, lighter, and quite dry. Shake off the talcum powder. Unpin the cotton tape and get decorating! I've used left-over bits of ribbon and braid. Glue or pin them into place. (By the way, if you use pins, keep the pomander away from the baby.) When you've finished, you'll have an attractive scented pomander which will make an ideal present. And if you put a loop on top, you can hang it on the Christmas tree, all ready to give on Christmas Day.

CHRISTMAS GLITTER

These cards are very simple to make, and cheap, too. Apart from the card and glue, you only need a few short pieces of tinsel and scraps of foil. For extra sparkle, finish off the cards with some glitter, if your pocket money allows!

First choose your envelopes. Cut your cards to fit the envelope *when folded in half*. Near the bottom of the card, stick on a tub shape cut from a scrap of coloured foil—a sweet paper or milk bottle top will do.

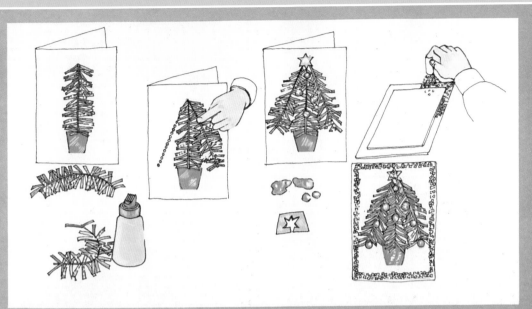

For the tree itself you'll need three pieces of green tinsel. Put a line of glue up from the centre of the tub nearly to the top—leaving room for the star. Stick on your first piece of tinsel, slightly overlapping the edge of the tub. Glue the other two pieces on either side with the top ends meeting and the bottom ends spread out. Make sure all the strands of tinsel are pointing in a *downwards* direction. Trim off any straggly ends to make the tree a good shape.

Decorations
Cut out a small star from gold or silver foil and glue at the top of the tree. Crumple up small pieces of coloured foil into flattish, round shapes and glue on tree. To trim the edges of the card with glitter, cover the main part of the card with paper, leaving just a narrow edge showing all round. Put clear glue on to this edge, shake glitter over it. Shake the ''spare'' glitter off on to a bit of newspaper and use again. Put glitter on the star, too.

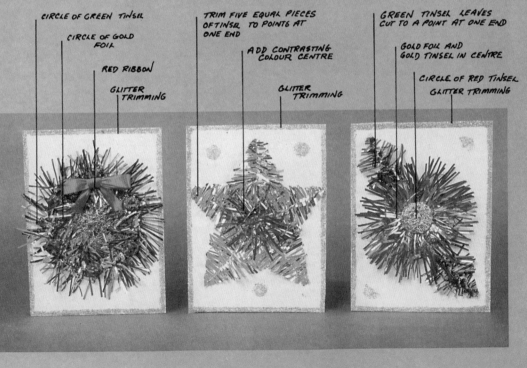

CIRCLE OF GREEN TINSEL
CIRCLE OF GOLD FOIL
RED RIBBON
GLITTER TRIMMING

TRIM FIVE EQUAL PIECES OF TINSEL TO POINTS AT ONE END
ADD CONTRASTING COLOUR CENTRE
GLITTER TRIMMING

GREEN TINSEL LEAVES CUT TO A POINT AT ONE END
GOLD FOIL AND GOLD TINSEL IN CENTRE
CIRCLE OF RED TINSEL
GLITTER TRIMMING

CHRISTMAS GARLANDS

Here's an idea for something you can make in a jiffy if you're short of a decoration or two at Christmas. As well as being quick and easy, it's a real money saver, and although you *can* use coloured paper, a white garland looks very snowy and winterish.

For one garland, all you need is: A few bits of tinsel and ribbon, a piece of kitchen foil, a bit of stiff garden wire (or a *thin* wire coat hanger) and three sheets of tissue paper. Bend the wire into a circle to make the frame.

GLUE

Leaves

1 Mark one sheet of the tissue paper in squares of about 10 cm. Put the other two sheets underneath and cut out all three sheets at once.

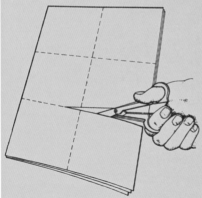

2 Shape each square over a finger, pulling the paper round the finger with your other hand.

3 Push the wire through the flattened end of each leaf – about 1 cm from the end – and thread all the leaves on to the frame. (Stick a cork or a piece of sticky tape on one end of the wire to stop them falling off.)

4 Add the leaves until the frame is thickly covered, leaving just a short piece of wire at each end. You'll get a nice rounded shape if you alternate the points of the leaves so that one points inwards and the next outwards etc. as you push them on.

5 When the frame's full, push the last few leaves on either side down and bind the ends of the wire together with sticky tape. Make a hook from a short piece of wire and tape it on securely, making sure it's a big one, otherwise the garland won't hang properly.

STICKY TAPE

6 Ease the leaves back again, close to the sticky tape, and hide the hook with a large bow from gift ribbon held on with tape or fuse wire. (If you're no good at big bows, make three or four small ones with long ends and fasten them together.)

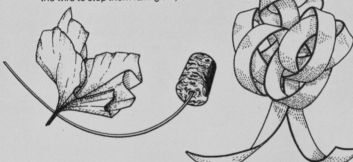

Flowers

7 Make seven of these, using 7 circles of kitchen foil shaped over your finger like the leaves. Complete the centre of each flower with a dab of glue and a piece of tinsel.

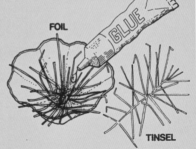

FOIL

GLUE

TINSEL

Glue the flower onto the garland. If you've run out of kitchen foil, milk bottle tops are just as good, but you'll need more, as they're small. For a finishing touch, glue tiny scraps of tinsel in the spaces *between* the flowers and get an extra Christmas sparkle!

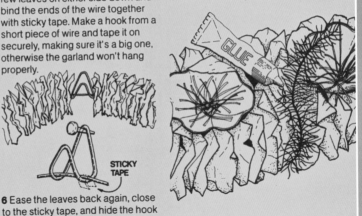

Cool Christmas

Trees

If you want a Christmas tree with a difference, follow these instructions and you'll end up with something cool and stylish. And you can pack this tree away and bring it out year after year – how green is that? The colour scheme is entirely up to you. If you want a metallic finish, gold or silver enamel paint looks good.

You will need:

Large cardboard boxes
Cardboard tubes of various sizes
Masking tape
Paper
All-purpose glue
Paint (acrylic, enamel, poster or tester pots of emulsion)
Christmas bauble
Ruler
Scissors
Pencil

1 Cut strips of corrugated cardboard from a box. All the strips should be 3.5 cm wide. Measure and cut three strips that are 78 cm long and make a bend on all three strips at roughly 22 cm. This section will form the base.

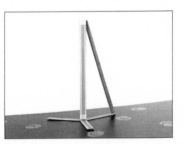

2 Stand the three strips together to form a triangle and wrap masking tape around the top and bottom to secure them in place. Cover the cut edges of the strips with masking tape or sticky paper. It has to be paper to ensure a good painting surface.

3 Measure the distance from the end of the base to the top of your tree, and cut three strips to this length. Attach them at the top and the base with masking tape.

4 Cut three shorter strips that will become horizontals between the centre and the slanted strips. We cut ours 22 cm long. Score 2 cm at each end of the strips and peel back the top layer of paper so they can be glued in place.

5 Glue the horizontal strips a little way up from the base – roughly 6 cm – sticking the paper ends downwards onto the upright strips. When the glue has dried, you can paint the tree shape.

6 Cut the cardboard tubes into 3.5 cm wide pieces. Arrange them roughly in your structure. When you have cut enough to fill the tree, remove and paint them.

7 Paint the outsides of the tubes to match the tree but paint the insides in a variety of colours. Another variation is to paint the tree bright pink and inside the tubes white.

8 Put the tubes back in place, gluing where they touch the frame and each other. Top off your cool Christmas tree with a pretty bauble, glued into position.

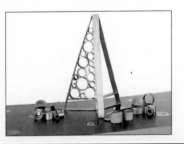

An Hachette UK Company
www.hachette.co.uk

First published in Great Britain in 2018 by
Kyle Books, an imprint of Kyle Cathie Ltd
Carmelite House, 50 Victoria Embankment
London, EC4Y 0DZ
www.kylebooks.com

ISBN: 978 0 85783 513 0

Publisher: Joanna Copestick
Editorial Director: Judith Hannam
Editorial Assistant: Isabel Gonzalez-Prendergast
Designer: Louise Leffler
Production: Caroline Alberti & Lisa Pinnell

A Cataloguing in Publication record for this title
is available from the British Library.

Printed and bound in China

10 9 8 7 6 5 4 3 2 1

Note: This book contains projects that no longer comply with current health and safety
standards and are for information only. The publishers and BBC cannot be held responsible
for claims arising from the inappropriate use of potentially hazardous materials.